Critical Years at the Yard

by the same author

★

DOUBLE DETECTION
(*Longmans*)

INSPECTOR BURMANN'S BUSIEST DAY
(*Longmans*)

THE SECRET OF SUPT. MANNING
(*Longmans*)

NO CHARGE FOR THE POISON
(*Methuen*)

THE LUNATIC, THE LOVER
(*Methuen*)

NO MERCY FOR MARGARET
(*Methuen*)

NEXT-DOOR TO DEATH
(*Methuen*)

DETECTIVE IN DISTRESS
(*Methuen*)

CORPSE INCOGNITO
(*Methuen*)

NEED A BODY TELL?
(*W. H. Allen*)

THE WILLING WITNESS
(*W. H. Allen*)

DRINK ALONE AND DIE
(*W. H. Allen*)

CORPSE AT CASABLANCA
(*W. H. Allen*)
(*in the press*)

Picture Post Library

SUPT. WILLIAMSON
OF THE DETECTIVE DEPARTMENT

"A modest man with a sense of humour"

Critical Years at the Yard

The Career of
Frederick Williamson
of the Detective Department
and the C.I.D.

by

BELTON COBB

FABER AND FABER
24 Russell Square
London

First published in mcmlvi
by Faber & Faber Limited
24 *Russell Square London W.C.*1
Printed in Great Britain by
Purnell and Sons Limited
Paulton (Somerset) and London

To

PHEBE

daughter and friend

Foreword

On the shelves of the London Library, where books are so admirably classified under subjects, there is a small section of books on CRIME, a still smaller section on POLICE—and a quite enormous section on CRIMINAL TRIALS.

Of the making of books, nowadays, on the absorbing subject of crime there is certainly no end. In the great majority of them—apart, of course, from the fictional stories—the interest hangs on the question of whether the arrested man will be found guilty and sentenced, or whether he will be acquitted. The reason for this would appear to be, not that the writers of the books regard that as the only interesting point in a crime story, but that the trial records are the easiest sources of information. It seems to be thought that until the prisoner reaches the dock there is not very much known about a crime.

There are, however, other sources of information for those who take the trouble to hunt for them. In particular, the newspapers of the Victorian age very frequently did something which no newspaper would do nowadays: in describing what they almost invariably referred to as 'atrocious crimes', they gave details of the day-by-day activities of the detectives, and recounted each speculative police theory as it was held, abandoned, and replaced by the next one.

It is thus possible to piece together the stories—surely the far more interesting stories—of how the criminals came to be suspected, how the evidence was built up against them, and how they were arrested. In other words, instead of giving accounts of mainly forensic interest, we are able to produce real-life detective stories.

When a book is based on trial reports, we see the accused, the judge, counsel and witnesses. We hear, rather vaguely, of 'the police' without getting any idea of the individual policeman concerned; although they have been, up to that point, the leading actors in a drama, they remain generally anonymous. They seem to be part of an institution rather than living men.

Intensive search into the records, however, shows us the names of the detectives and something of their characters and methods of work. We can trace which detectives were concerned with each particular case. We can follow these detectives, as real men, throughout their careers.

. . . . .

The period of thirty years in the history of Scotland Yard, which forms the subject of this book, was one of intense drama, not merely because of particular crimes, but also because of events which threatened to disrupt the entire existence of the newly-created Metropolitan Police Force. During those years, certain detectives rose to high rank and then—in one way or another—failed and were disgraced. They very nearly dragged the police down with them. The fact that they did not, and that Scotland Yard continued and became firmly established, is tribute to other detectives who—as was said in an obituary notice of the most long-standing and remarkable of them—showed 'special shrewdness, unerring judgement, unswerving integrity and perfect trustworthiness'.

Here, then, amid the story of the Detective Department of the Metropolitan Police (which later became the Criminal Investigation Department), is the record of the individual men—the great detectives and the lesser detectives—who fought against crime in London for thirty years: and the record of one, Frederick Williamson, in particular.

Contents

I.

THE FIRST CRISIS

II.

SEQUEL TO THE FIRST CRISIS

III.

THE SECOND CRISIS

IV.

SEQUEL TO THE SECOND CRISIS

V.

THE THIRD CRISIS

VI.

SEQUEL TO THE THIRD CRISIS

VII.

THE FOURTH CRISIS

Illustrations

PART ONE

The First Crisis

CHAPTER 1

The Detective Department

1

The Metropolitan Police were created by Sir Robert Peel in 1829.

Before that, there had only been about 1,000 policemen, of all sorts, in London, and of those only 189 were paid. Seeing that it was estimated that there were 30,000 thieves, it is not surprising that 'offences against property have of late increased . . . and the establishments of nightly watch and nightly police have been found inadequate to the prevention and detection of crime'.

Peel's new police were to remedy that state of affairs. The Force was to consist of over 3,000 men, all paid (£50 a year for a constable and £200 a year for a superintendent), and there were to be 17 divisions, from Kensington to Whitechapel and from Hampstead to Southwark.

When it came to recruiting, about a third of the men were unskilled labourers, one-sixth were from the armed forces, and the remainder were skilled workmen—but presumably unemployed and possibly unemployable—

from gentlemen's servants to weavers, from butchers and bakers to bricklayers and blacksmiths. It must have been a motley crew, and many of its members were quite unsuitable for the work—as is shown by the fact that the personnel was constantly changing. In the process of keeping up a strength of 3,000 men, in the first eight years no less than 5,000 men were dismissed after enlistment, while nearly 6,000 more resigned, either voluntarily or under persuasion.

The 17 Divisions were denominated, as at present, by letters of the alphabet, but this arrangement was not precisely the one that has survived. In particular, A Division was not, as is now the case, responsible for the patrolling of Westminster; it consisted entirely of the 'Headquarters Staff'. In the buildings at Great Scotland Yard[1] and Whitehall Place were 100 men, working in various Departments, including the Executive Department of the Commissioners' Office, the Accounts Department, the Criminal Returns Office, and the Detective Department.

2

Originally, the Force was under the control of two Commissioners, Mr. Richard Mayne and Colonel Charles Rowan.[2] They worked together for twenty-one years, and then, in 1850, Rowan retired owing to ill-health. Then, for another eighteen years, Mayne carried on alone, with first one and then two Assistant-Commissioners under him. Thus at the period when this chronicle starts, Sir Richard Mayne was in indisputable authority over the police.

[1] About 200 yards north of the present New Scotland Yard.
[2] They were both made K.C.B.s between 1848 and 1851.

Mayne was an enthusiast with tremendous energy and determination. The Metropolitan Police was his life-work, and in a sense he loved it and everyone in it. At any rate, he always fought against detractors of his men, whether they were private individuals, Members of Parliament, the newspapers, or government officials. To hear him speak, outside his own office, one would have thought that the Force was composed of geniuses and saints.

Inside his office, however, he was completely realistic, being apparently of the opinion that (as, indeed, was probably to a considerable extent the case in the first years) 'a lot of scallywags' would be a more fitting description of his men. Yet if that was so—or in so far as it was so—it was never his fault. He was continually driving out the goats, and keeping the sheep only on probation in case any of them should grow horns. And when that metamorphosis occurred, he was entirely ruthless, with no mercy for first offenders and taking no account of 'past meritorious services'. He frequently issued orders against drunkenness, for instance, and on one occasion, at Christmas time, he decreed that any man reported to him for that offence should be dismissed from the Force; and when about sixty men were reported, he did dismiss them all, although some of them had served under him for twenty years.

He was, indeed, a hard man. He had 'a very hard, compressed mouth' and 'an eye like that of a hawk'. Discipline meant everything to him, and sentiment nothing. Though in one sense he loved his police force, he knew no one in it as a human being, his only 'friend' among the several thousand men under his command being his personal clerk. He never relaxed, and he never spoke an unnecessary word.

It is recorded that interviews with him were always painful. When a subordinate was summoned to his room to be reprimanded, the effect was like that of being annihilated by an iceberg. And even when the purpose of the interview was a favourable one—such as an announcement of promotion—the atmosphere was almost equally chilling; for several minutes Sir Richard would continue to write at his desk without looking up, while the subordinate waited in dreadful uncertainty as to whether he was there to be promoted or dismissed—then Mayne would look up and say, 'Ah, Sergeant Williamson. I have decided that you shall be promoted inspector. Good day to you.'

3

Such a man would necessarily keep all the affairs of the Force directly under his own control. Indeed, for many years Mayne insisted that all letters received by superintendents of the Divisions should be passed to him for reply.

But, up to about the year 1860, he made one exception to that. The Detective Department appears to have escaped from some of the rigours of his supervision.

There were several reasons for that.

For one thing, it was at first a very small department. The authorities differ as to the precise number of men employed in it, the fact being that arrangements at Great Scotland Yard were somewhat fluid, and the departments tended to overlap; thus in times of pressure the inspector of the Excutive Department of the Commissioners' Office was called upon to assist the two inspectors of the Detective Department. Officially, the number of men in

SIR RICHARD MAYNE

"He had a very hard, compressed mouth and an eye like that of a hawk"

that Department was only 8, though there were probably 12 sharing the work.

Then, although Mayne never suffered from any lack of self-confidence, he must have known that he was no expert in detection. It is true that, at the start, he was no 'expert' in creating a police force, being a barrister with six years' practice at the Bar. But he had qualities, which Sir Robert Peel recognised, that entirely fitted him for that work.[1] His combination of energy and ruthlessness made the Force a success. Detection, however, required more than mere energy; it could not be done—or even directed—without very considerable technical knowledge.

That knowledge lay, very completely, with the two inspectors who led the Detective Department in its earliest years. They both had had vast experience, and it must therefore have seemed to Mayne that matters could safely be left in their hands. He would assign one or other of them to a particular case, and then rest contented until he heard that the matter had been solved and the criminal arrested.

It was not until after 1860 that he began to have doubts of the wisdom of letting even that much of the work go out of his own hands.

4

In the 1850's, the two inspectors of the Detective Department were Stephen Thornton and Jonathan Whicher. Both men had been in the Department ever since its

[1] It was thought necessary for one Commissioner to be a soldier—to ensure action—and for the other to be a lawyer—to keep the action within legal bounds.

creation in 1842. That implies that they had been trained by the last of the Bow Street Runners.

Before the days of the Runners, criminals were either caught red-handed, or 'sold' by their friends or enemies (who were rewarded with £40)—or else they went scot-free, for the time being. Nothing was ever done—indeed, it was not realised that anything could be done—to trace a criminal once he had got away.

The Runners, when they took up the work of 'thief-catching', started the science of detection as opposed to the mere practice of 'the hue and cry'. They were not content to wait for information to be brought to them, they went out to look for it, sometimes even disguising themselves and living amongst the criminals to hear their secrets. By doing so, they learnt very much about criminals and their ways, as well as about particular crimes, and they began a system of tabulating the information they had obtained.

When the Metropolitan Police was formed, it was realised that although you could start from scratch in training a police constable, even if you had never trained one before—provided you knew the effect you wanted to get—you couldn't train a detective without knowing how that particular work was done. Some of the more trustworthy of the Runners were therefore allowed to continue for thirteen years while the new police studied their methods.

The earliest detectives of the Metropolitan Police thus learnt all that the Runners knew, and then developed their own ideas, particularly about looking for 'clues' and deducing facts from them. At first that meant no more than being able to tell, from signs left on the scene of a crime, whether it had been committed by inexperienced men or by old thieves. But within a few years—as in the case of the murder of Lord William Russell—the new detectives could analyse the clues and defeat the most ingenious efforts of criminals to lay false trails.

Stephen Thornton and Jonathan Whicher were among those men who worked out the principles of the new science.

5

In one of his articles in *Household Words*, Charles Dickens wrote: 'The Detective Force organised since the establishment of the existing police is so well chosen and trained, proceeds so systematically and quietly, does its business in such a workmanlike manner, and is always so calmly and steadily engaged in the service of the public, that the public really do not know enough of it, to know a tithe of its usefulness. Impressed with this conviction, and interested in the men themselves, we represented to the authorities at Scotland Yard that we should be glad, if there were no official objection, to have some talk with the Detectives.'

As a result of those overtures, two inspectors and five sergeants came to be interviewed—and thus to be immortalised by Charles Dickens. They were not, as it happened, all from the Detective Department—another example of the over-lapping system in the Commissioners' Office. But what is of importance and value to us is that two of the sergeants were Stephen Thornton and Jonathan Whicher.[1]

[1] Dickens chose to disguise the actual names. Thornton appears as 'Dornton' and Whicher as 'Witchem'. The article is included in *Reprinted Pieces*.

'They sit down in a semi-circle (the two inspectors at the two ends) at a little distance from the round table, facing the editorial sofa. Every man of them, at a glance, immediately takes an inventory of the furniture and an accurate sketch of the editorial presence. The editor feels that any gentleman in company could take him up, if need be, without the smallest hesitation, twenty years hence.

'The whole party are in plain clothes. Sergeant Dornton, about fifty years of age, with a ruddy face and a high sun-burnt forehead, has the air of one who has been a sergeant in the army. . . . He is famous for steadily pursuing the inductive process, and, from small beginnings, working up from clue to clue until he bags his man. Sergeant Witchem, shorter and thicker-set, and marked with the small-pox, has something of a reserved and thoughtful air, as if he were engaged in deep arithmetical calculations.'

By the 1860's, all the detectives whom Dickens interviewed had died or retired, except those two, Stephen Thornton and Jonathan Whicher. They had both become inspectors, and the responsibility for the Department rested in their hands.

But whereas Inspector Thornton was by then an elderly man, near the time of retirement, Inspector Whicher was still in the prime of life. Even Sir Richard Mayne—who was so lavish with blame and so extremely sparing with praise—thought well of him. His record of successes in criminal cases was supreme. It is said of him: 'Whicher was, indeed, an excellent officer, quiet, shrewd, and practically never in a hurry, generally successful, and ready to take on any case';[1] while another man who had

[1] Inspector Arthur Lansdowne.

worked under him[1] calls him, 'The prince of detectives. . . . The best detective Scotland Yard ever possessed.'

6

As this record covers a period of nearly thirty years, it is necessarily the younger men who will come nearest to surviving through its pages: the men who, in the 1860's, were not yet above the rank of sergeant.

The oldest of them was George Clarke, who had joined the Metropolitan Police as a constable in 1840. He had married young, and had a wife and child when most of the other sergeants were living in 'single men's quarters' at No. 1, Palace Place, Great Scotland Yard. He would appear to have been a 'good sort', dependable (up to a point) and highly intelligent; but for some unexplained reason he did not get quick promotion—it was only after 28 years of service that he reached the rank of inspector.

William Palmer was in the Force by 1847 and became an inspector after 21 years. It is doubtful if he had great intelligence or orginality; but he was the solid, perhaps stolid, type who kept all the conventions and would 'never let his side down'.

Richard Tanner started as a constable in C Division in 1850, at the age of 20, and transferred to the Detective Department in 1855 as a 'clerk'. He was a lively youngster, with (as is recorded by his contemporaries) a habit of 'making a book' on the chances of any important event such as promotions or the allotment of particular cases. He did well, for he became an inspector only eight years after joining the Department. Unhappily, he died young

[1] Chief Inspector Tim Cavanagh.

(at the age of 41), but he left his mark in the history of Scotland Yard over one famous case.

Nathaniel Druscovich did not join the Department until 1864, but—probably because he had the gift of languages and could thus become a 'specialist'—he became an inspector within five years. The word for him is 'smart'; he appears to have been particularly smart in appearance as well as in character.

There was a Sergeant Thomas (Christian name unknown), who figured in various cases up to 1865; but he never became an inspector.

Finally, to complete the set of six sergeants and two inspectors, there was Adolphus Frederick Williamson. Of him much more is known than of any of the others. He was at Scotland Yard during practically the whole of our period, starting as an assistant clerk in the Detective Department and ending as Chief Constable of its successor, the Criminal Investigation Department. In so far as this chronicle has a central figure, that figure is Frederick Williamson.

7

Williamson's father was a native of Perthshire, who became a warrant officer in the Royal Artillery and fought at Waterloo. A dour Scot, perhaps, and a disciplinarian. At any rate, when the Metropolitan Police was formed, he was one of the 17 men immediately picked for the office of Superintendent; he was put in charge of T Division, with his headquarters at Hammersmith.

There, two years later, Frederick Williamson was born; there, he grew up amongst policemen and acquired an ambition to be one himself, and a Superintendent in due course.

When he was 17, after education at Hammersmith Grammar School, he appears to have got his father to pull strings to get him into a good job. The son of a warrant officer in the artillery could get an entry into the War Office, and accordingly Frederick Williamson started there, as a 'temporary clerk' in the Ordnance Department. It may be imagined that the only thing he liked about that clerkship was its temporariness; for it did not lead towards the fulfilment of the ambition. So when he was 19, more strings were pulled, and he became an assistant clerk in the Metropolitan Police. From there, he somehow worked his way into the Detective Department. A few years later, he was promoted sergeant.

In those days, Frederick Williamson showed a double character. He won the sobriquet of 'Dolly' (a contraction, of course, of Adolphus) and was altogether a very bright young spark. He 'was possessed of a considerable amount of dry humour and chaff. . . . Scarcely a "barney"' (or, as we would now say, 'a rag') 'was got up that he was not in, but he had a happy knack of keeping out of trouble, when some of the others easily got spotted'.[1] On the other hand, his ambition always remained before him (and perhaps that was why he kept out of trouble, since the iron hand of Mr. Mayne, who did not even possess any velvet gloves, still fell drastically on any man who proved unsatisfactory). His ambition kept him always thinking of the future. 'When we had finished our day's work at the desk, preparatory to going to the theatres at night, we wanted a spell of rest and fresh air. . . . When we reached home from the theatres, etc., we generally congregated in the little parlour and kitchen, chatting about events generally, or having a game of loo. . . . Dolly Williamson possessed

[1] Chief Inspector Tim Cavanagh.

good shrewd commonsense, and while we were at the theatres or other places of entertainment he passed his time of an evening learning French. His tutor was in the French colony near Leicester Square'.[1]

Somehow or other, these studious habits did not detract from Williamson's popularity. No doubt he did go to the theatres now and then. He was good company at dinners given to celebrate successful 'barneys' and would always oblige with a song. He was skilful at sculling on the river. And he was in love with a girl named Emma Macpherson.[2]

Without a doubt, he got all the enjoyment he could out of life, in spite of the ambition.

8

Thus the personnel of the Detective Department at Great Scotland Yard in 1860 consisted of Inspector Thornton and Inspector Whicher, Sergeant Williamson, Sergeant Tanner, Sergeant Thomas, Sergeant Palmer, Sergeant Clarke and one other—probably a Sergeant Robinson who very soon disappeared from the records. The inspectors were responsible, amongst other things, for the training of the sergeants; but with so small a staff it was impossible for cases—except those of particular importance—to be handled by more than one man, so most of the instruction was by precept rather than by example. Nevertheless each inspector applied himself to the training of a particular group of sergeants, and each inspector had his favourites. Frederick Williamson was certainly the favourite sergeant of Inspector Whicher—a

[1] Chief Inspector Tim Cavanagh.
[2] Whom he eventually married.

fact on which much of the early history of this period depends.

It is with Inspector Whicher and Sergeant Williamson—and of course the Commissioner, Sir Richard Mayne—that this chronicle opens.

CHAPTER 2

Child Murder

1

On July 3rd, 1860, *The Times* reported that 'A shocking murder was perpetrated at Road, a village four miles from Frome, on Saturday morning last'. Eight days later, *The Morning Post* said of the same crime, 'A murder has just been committed which for mystery, complication of probabilities and hideous wickedness is without parallel in our criminal records.'

Twelve people had slept in the house at Road on that Friday night . . . or, to be more exact, ten had slept, one had been murdered, and one had stayed awake to do the killing. Mr. and Mrs. Kent had slept in one room with a little girl of 5. Two grown-up daughters by Mr. Kent and his first wife had been together in another room. Two other children of the first family—Constance, aged 16, and William, aged 15—had had rooms to themselves. The cook and housemaid had shared a room. And the nurse had been in the nursery with Francis, aged 4½, and a little girl, aged 2.

It was the little boy in the nursery who was shockingly murdered.

According to the nurse's statement, she had lit a nightlight at 11.0 and had looked at the boy in the cot a few minutes later, before getting into her own bed. The mother had seen the nursery door ajar at some time between 11.0 and 12.0 and had shut it. No sounds had been heard during the night.

At 5 a.m., the nurse (again according to her own statement) had awakened and seen that the boy's cot was empty. That had not alarmed her, she said, because she thought the mother must have been in and have carried him to her own room. She therefore went to sleep again. She awoke once more at 6.15 and then she noticed that the nursery door was open, which seemed to confirm that the mother had been in, as she had heard it shut the night before. She got up then, and it was while she was dressing that she remembered that the mother was within a week or two of delivery of another child and would probably not have been able to pick the boy out of a high-sided cot. At 6.40, therefore, when she was dressed, she knocked on the door of the mother's room, 'just to make sure'. There was no answer, and she did not like to disturb her mistress. She did not do any more (she said) till 7.30, when she knocked again and found Mrs. Kent awake—and learnt that the boy was not in his mother's room.

A search for him was then started. He was nowhere in the house, but eventually—after an hour—his dead body was found in the pan of an outside privy, 25 feet from the house. His throat had been cut from ear to ear.

2

It was established from the first, by the reasoning of the County Constabulary, that the murder could not have been committed by anyone outside the house . . . 'the guilty person must have been in the house overnight'. Obviously, the murderer was not either of the two smallest children, both of who were under 5 years old, and it was confirmed by medical opinion that Mrs. Kent would have been incapable of lifting the boy from the cot and carrying him out of the house. Thus the number of people on the 'suspect list' was reduced to eight; Mr. Kent, the two grown-up daughters, William and Constance, the nurse, the cook and the housemaid.

The horrors of this crime brought it enormous public attention. The newspapers of that day were remarkably outspoken. One paper, for instance, demanded that a *cordon judiciare* should be drawn round the house and that the occupants should be confined within it 'till the truth is found'. The same paper, in an extraordinary leading article on the crime, openly hinted at the guilt of the father, Mr. Kent—'Thus much is certain, then, that the murderer was either a man, a woman, or one of the big children. If a man, there was but one.'[1]

Other opinion fixed the guilt, with equal frankness, on the nurse, Elizabeth Gough, who certainly appeared to have had the best opportunity of removing the child from his cot.

The local Constabulary appear to have been at their wits' end, and much disturbed by receiving too much advice over a problem which appeared to them to be inexplicable. It can be understood that police officials who had never been trained as detectives and had had no experience of major crime would have been thrown off their balance by the 'complication of probabilities' and by being told that 'The sacredness of English households

[1] *The Morning Post.*

demands that this matter shall never be allowed to rest till the last shadow in the dark mystery shall have been cleared away by the light of unquestionable truth'.[1]

In such a situation, the need was for action. People and newspapers were howling for an arrest; so, nearly a fortnight after the discovery of the crime, the nursemaid was 'apprehended on suspicion'.

There was never much evidence—if any—against her, so that 'A very general impression of the nursemaid's innocence exists out of doors, and, in fact, one of the police engaged in the investigation of the case stated his belief that there was nothing to warrant her detention'.[2] Nevertheless, to some minds, arrest in a criminal matter implies guilt, and even in those days there were amateur theorists, so 'a report was widely spread' that the nursemaid had confessed to an intrigue between Mr. Kent and herself, as a result of which (though what was the necessity for it was not stated) the father had murdered his own child, with the knowledge and connivance of his *inamorata.* 'There is not,' said *The Times*, 'the shadow of foundation for any such statement.'

Elizabeth Gough, however, was held in custody while enquiries continued. It was found that the privy in which the body was found was built over an open cess-pool, and it was concluded that the murderer's intention was that the body should fall through and completely disappear. To support that theory—and this was the one piece of intelligent detection done by the local Constabulary, even if its implications were not seen, and it was not followed-up—it was learnt that some three years before, Constance Kent (then aged 13) had hidden her

[1] *The Morning Post.*
[2] *The Times.*

clothes in that privy when she had disguised herself as a boy and run away from home with her brother William.

3

The outcry over the case, and the plain statements that the police were showing their inefficiency, became so prominent that the Home Secretary was forced to intervene.

In the days of the Bow Street Runners, private individuals could 'hire' a Runner for work in the provinces, usually with an eye, not so much to the arrest of a criminal, as to the recovery of stolen property. The Metropolitan Police discontinued that practice, and when their establishment was followed by that of the County Constabularies the different forces worked quite independently, there being no system by which the London Police could handle cases outside their own area. Here, however, the reputation of 'Peel's New Police' as a whole was at stake and likely to crumble unless experienced detectives took a hand in the matter. The Home Secretary therefore approached Sir Richard Mayne with the suggestion (though it was probably an order) that his best detective should be sent to Road.

Accordingly, Mayne selected Inspector Jonathan Whicher for the task.

4

In the time of the Fieldings (who started the Bow Street Runners) the police were nothing more than officers of the magistrates.[1] Outside London, that system con-

[1] Readers of *The Pickwick Papers* will recall how Mr. Nupkins, the magistrate, 'rushed into a prize-ring on the fourth of May last . . . attended by only sixty special constables'; and the relations between Mr. Nupkins and Grummer, the constable.

tinued for many years, the magistrates in some districts fulfilling the functions now done by Chief Constables. Thus, in this enquiry into the death of Francis Saville Kent, the local Constabulary were answerable to a body of local magistrates (including the Vicar), and even Inspector Whicher 'of the Metropolitan Detective Police' had to work very closely in with them. Therefore Whicher's first act on reaching Trowbridge, even before he visited the scene of the crime, was to have an interview with the magistrates. They, no doubt, welcomed him warmly as someone who was going to relieve them of unpleasant responsibilities.

They must, indeed, have been an extremely uncomfortable body of men.

Notoriety had been thrust upon them. They were being publicly challenged as inefficient if not incompetent. And they were faced with all those rumours, on which they saw no grounds to act, against Mr. Kent—who was a gentleman and almost the Squire of his village, who sat in a front pew at the church, and who was personally known to them and respected by them. There were rumours, too, against members of Mr. Kent's family. And one of his servants was still held in custody, not because there was any evidence against her, but because to set her free would imply a mistake on the part of the police (and thus on the part of the magistrates) and would show that the mystery was no nearer to solution than it had been when it started, three weeks before.

Jonathan Whicher, however, had a manner which inspired confidence. There was no longer any need for the magistrates to be concerned; now that it was in his hands, the case would very soon be solved and all the trouble ended. The nursemaid, he said, must be set free at once, any outcry resulting from her release being sure to be counterbalanced by the announcement that a real detective was now dealing with the case. In a very few days. . . .

And in fact it was only four days later that Inspector Whicher went to the magistrates again. He must then have startled and disturbed them very much. For he demanded the issue of a warrant for the arrest of Constance, Mr. Kent's 16-year-old daughter.

5

It took Whicher four hours of argument to get that warrant. The magistrates issued it eventually, but most unwillingly. This was far, far worse than arresting a nursemaid.

When Whicher executed the warrant and put Constance under arrest, the girl cried out, 'Oh, no, no. I am innocent, I am innocent.' Nevertheless, the magistrates, having gone so far as to issue the warrant, could do nothing but remand her, and she was removed to Devizes Gaol.

Inspector Whicher had had very little evidence to go on. Indeed, he appears to have acted on the strength of a theory of the case and what would now be called a 'hunch'. In his own mind, he was sure of Constance Kent's guilt: but he had, as yet, no proof of it—certainly he had nothing that would convince a jury at the trial.

He now had to get the evidence during the week's remand, in order to be sure that the hesitating magistrates would commit the case to the Assizes.

He therefore telegraphed to Sir Richard Mayne, requesting the services of an assistant. He asked specifically for Sergeant Williamson, or, failing him, for Sergeant Tanner.

Meanwhile, he set to work on his own, with—as *The Times* reported on July 23rd—'his wonted sagacity'.

Two days later, it was announced that 'Sergeant Williamson, of the Metropolitan Detective Force, has arrived in Road and is actively engaged with Mr. Inspector Whicher in investigating this tragic affair'.

CHAPTER 3

Detectives at Work

1

Inspector Whicher would have explained the position when Frederick Williamson congratulated him on the arrest. . . .

'Thankee, my boy, thankee. These things aren't so difficult when you've my amount of experience. You get to see things, know things, feel 'em in your bones. I come here and I take one look at the people, and I'm sure who's done it. Not a doubt. No use troubling about Mr. Kent or that nursemaid or any of the others, because I don't feel anything about them. But this Constance, for all she's no more than a child, she's different. She's got a watchful look about her, and I know why: she's afraid. And at the same time she's hiding all the cunning there is in her: she's trying to make herself look stupid and dull —only she ain't stupid and she ain't dull. Not a bit of it.[1]

'Now, there's two things we've got to find, and find quickly. The first is why she did it, and the second is

[1] This is based on a report on the prisoner's appearance which appeared in the *Daily Telegraph*. In general, Whicher's 'idiom' is based on Dickens' record of his speech.

proof that she did it. I've some ideas already on *why* she did it. It's what you'd expect, in a family like that with two parts to it, as you might say. The father, first of all, has a wife and four children. Then the wife dies and he gets a new wife and starts having more children. Very nice for the first lot, you might say, having babies to play with; only they don't take it that way. Might be all right if there was only one, they'd get used to him; but when it's a new one a year, almost, that's different. They say, "Father, why don't you take us fishing like you used to do?" and he says, "Run along now, I'm busy playing with my new baby." More or less like that, you know, even if he doesn't do all that playing with children. There'd be jealousy, naturally. But we've got to prove that. There's a bit of evidence already, found before I came along but not taken much notice of: that's Constance and William Kent running off three years ago, she with her hair cut off and dressed up like a boy, because they weren't happy at home. Stands to reason, that—children don't run off when it's a nice home and all's well, so there must have been trouble.

'Well, that's something to start on. But we want more, we've got to get evidence as to what that trouble was. It was the jealousy, of course, but we've got to prove that. We've got to find that this girl Constance told someone about her feelings. She did, of course, bound to have done. She'd have said a word or two to some of her school-mates, maybe. She's only 16, y'know, and she wouldn't have been able to keep a thing like that to herself.

'That's one thing we've got to do. The other will be more difficult, maybe. There's been a lot of cleaning-up in this house, since the murder. She stabbed the boy, so she must have used a knife; but all the knives in this house are where they ought to be, and clean at that. She carried the boy twenty-five feet from the house to that privy, but there aren't any soiled shoes. She must have used something pretty sharp for the throat-cutting, but there's nothing to be found. And there must have been bloodstains on her clothes, but they've all gone too.

'Well, that ain't natural. Particularly there not being any bloodstained clothing.

'Look at it this way. Sometime between 12.30 and 3.30 in the morning, that's when she did it. She mightn't have gone to bed first, and then she'd have had her clothes on when all the blood was splashing about. Or she might have gone to bed, and not dressed again, and then she'd have been in her nightdress. Or she could have gone to bed and dressed again afterwards, and then she'd have been in her clothes. One of the three, ain't it? Question is, which?

'Now, we know that, know it by reason, the way I know most things.

'She'd have gone to bed, to keep up appearances in case someone came in to say good night to her. Supposing one of her sisters had looked in—that being a custom in this house, I'm told—about eleven, say. Odd it would have looked, if she'd been up and all excited, and sharpening knives, wouldn't it?

'So we'll take it that she went to bed, pretending to be asleep. Then she got up again, say at 1 in the morning. Question is, did she put her clothes on again, or didn't she?

'Now, I'd say she didn't, because it would have looked odd if the nursemaid had wakened when she went into the nursery. "Oh, Miss Constance, what have you come for?" she'd say. And the girl'd answer, all innocent-sounding, "I just came to look at little Francis, because I didn't kiss him good night." Something like that, you know. And then the nursemaid would say, "Oh, but Miss Constance, you are all dressed in the middle of the night. Haven't you been to bed?"

'Odd, that would look, wouldn't it?

'So we'll take it that she wore her nightdress, all proper for the time of night, in case she was seen. Very well. Chilly it would have been, going out in the night like that, but maybe she'd have been thinking of something else and not have noticed. Anyway, that's what she'd have done. And then there'd have been blood, plenty of it, splashing on the nightdress: bound to have been some, anyway, however careful she was. So there is a nightdress somewhere that's got blood on it. May have been washed, I daresay it has, but there'll be enough on it still to be seen, blood not being so easy to get out.

"Well, there you are, Sergeant Williamson. That nightdress has disappeared. I've looked for it, and I'm pretty thorough. Question is, what has she done with it?"

2

Inspector Whicher would have had more to explain to Sergeant Williamson than that.

He had already begun enquiries about Constance Kent's nightdresses. The girl had had three—the housemaid had told him that. But only two of them could be found, one being under her pillow and the other having recently come back from the washerwoman. There was no trace of the third.

Before her arrest, Whicher had asked Constance herself about it, and had been told that it had been sent to the washerwoman and had not come back. When he pressed her for details about that, she said she had given it to the housemaid to be put into the soiled-linen basket. On the other hand, the washerwoman had told Whicher that none of Miss Constance's nightdresses had come to her that week: she had noticed especially, it being unusual for Miss Constance not to send one.

Whicher had not believed the obvious explanation that the washerwoman had stolen the nightdress—or had 'had an accident with it'—and was now telling lies to protect herself. He firmly believed that that nightdress had had bloodstains on it, and that it had been made to disappear in consequence. He accordingly had had a further talk with the housemaid. . . .

The housemaid remembered that morning perfectly well, because it was the one after that dreadful thing had happened to poor Master Francis. Everyone was that upset, what with what had happened and Mr. Morgan, the parish constable, being in the house and all. The mistress was ill with it, she being near her time, too, and the master didn't seem to know whether he ought to be with her or with Mr. Morgan; and Miss Mary and Miss Elizabeth had been crying, and—— Oh, it was a terrible time. But you had to get on with your work, hadn't you, and she had been trying to do the sweeping, because it was no good having the hysterics, like Cook. And then Miss Constance had called her and given her a nightdress and told her to put it into the soiled-linen basket. Which she had done, straight away.

After that, Whicher had got out of her that she had stayed on the landing for almost an hour—apparently because she was scared about being downstairs, where the body of poor Master Francis was being brought in after it was found and horrible things were happening. So she had stayed on the landing all that time—except when she slipped down to fetch the glass of water.

Thus it had all come out, very gradually and with much patience on Jonathan Whicher's part, that Miss Constance had come along the landing from her bedroom and had sent the housemaid to fetch her a glass of water; that when the housemaid left the landing, Miss Constance had remained standing close to the linen basket; and that Miss Constance had gone back to her bedroom by the time the glass of water was brought. . . .

'Well, there you are, Sergeant Williamson,' Inspector Whicher would have said. 'That's how she did it—this part of the business, anyhow. Neat, ain't it? She fixes the nightdress as having been put in the basket, and she's got a witness who'll swear it was there, and on the way to the washerwoman. No reason after that to suppose it didn't get there, is there? Then she feels faint, which anybody might in this house just then, and she needs a glass of water. Says she does, anyway, and sends the housemaid to get it. Why does she do it that way? Because the housemaid is lingering about and it would look odd if Miss Constance packed her off about her business without a reason, Miss Constance being only sixteen and not in the habit of giving that kind of order to the servants. Very anxious, Miss Constance is, not to do anything that would look odd. Then, as soon as the housemaid has gone downstairs, out comes the nightdress—bloodstains and all—from the basket, and it's taken back to Miss Constance's bedroom.

'Nice for me it would be, of course, if the housemaid had seen the bloodstains when she was putting the nightdress into the basket. But she didn't. I've asked her. It was all folded up, and, of course, she didn't open it out, why should she?

'Well, now. Question is, what happened to the nightdress after it was brought back to the bedroom? It isn't there, as it ought to be, so it has been put somewhere else. Question is, where?'

3

Jonathan Whicher's plan was that he and Sergeant Williamson should divide the work of that week, saving all the time they could because of the urgency of preparing a complete and convincing case against Constance Kent before the next sitting of the magistrates.

He himself would deal with the question of motive. The Sergeant's task was to find the missing nightdress. Maybe it had been buried, or maybe it had been burnt: but either way there'd be traces. There could be a reward offered, of as much as *5s.*, to anyone who could bring news of it.

But anyway it had to be found. Or bits of it, enough to prove that something had been done about destroying it, to show that Constance Kent was lying when she told that story about the linen basket.

CHAPTER 4

The Trial and its Sequel

1

'We are credibly informed,' said the *Western Morning News* on August 2nd, 'that Miss Constance Kent's demeanour in prison was calm and quiet, and that she appeared to be conscious of her innocence and ashamed of being placed in such a position.'

That calm demeanour she maintained in the Court Room. There were no more of the passionate tears which she had shed when Inspector Whicher arrested her. Instead, when she appeared before the magistrates, she looked very child-like and demure and innocent, just a little scared at finding herself in the dock but also surprised that anyone could have thought of putting her there.

If she had been instructed in her attitude, she could not have adopted one which would more greatly have helped her. For it emphasised the fact that she was a 'young lady', the daughter of that respected householder of the district, and not in any way the sort of person the magistrates were accustomed to having before them: while at the same time it appealed to their compassion by showing how cruel it was that a mere child of her age should be accused of dreadful crime.

2

There was, certainly, an array of evidence against her, marshalled skilfully by Inspector Whicher. However much embarrassed the magistrates may have felt—however much they may have wished that the person to be accused of this murder had been a vagrant or one of the village ne'er-do-wells—they could not deny that the Prosecution had a strong case against Constance Kent.

It became clear, as the case proceeded, that acute jealousy had been felt by the older family against the younger one—and shown particularly by the prisoner. Three years before, they were told, she had run away from home, because of that jealousy. More recently, she had spoken quite candidly of the feeling—Whicher produced two of her schoolmates to prove it. And to make the jealousy motive more plausible, evidence was given that the prisoner's mother had died in an asylum, her uncle had been in an asylum too: and, of course, if there was that kind of thing in the family it was perfectly possible—and reasonable—that even a child should have been turned by bitter jealousy to the state of mind which permitted such horrors as had been perpetrated.

Terrible as was the thought, the magistrates had to admit that the motive was established.

Then there was evidence to prove that the crime had actually been committed by the prisoner. Mostly, it turned on a strange story about a nightdress, which had been put in a basket to go to the washerwoman. . . .

As that story was unfolded in all its details, it must

have become clear that everything was going to hang on that. (If that phrase occurred to some of the magistrates, they may have thought grimly that it was Miss Constance Kent for whom a hanging was threatened: this child before them, this daughter of a respected householder. . . . If their consciences forced them to the dreadful act of committing her for trial, her ultimate fate would be practically certain.)

But if the Prosecution's claim that the prisoner had abstracted the nightdress from the soiled-linen basket were to be regarded as proved—if the magistrates were to believe that putting it there had been cunning deceit—if all this was to be accepted as having been done by the prisoner because there were blood-marks on the nightdress—then the nightdress must be produced in Court and the bloodstains seen.

Without that, there was nothing but an unsubstantiated theory. A plausible theory, maybe, but hardly a proved one.

3

The nightdress was not produced. The most diligent searches of Inspector Whicher and Sergeant Williamson, both of the Metropolitan Police Force, had failed to find it. And if they, with all their skill, could not find it. . . .

In cross-examination, the defending counsel had succeeded in making the evidence of the prisoner's two schoolmates look a little like schoolgirls' gossip: he had also shaken the evidence of the housemaid, and had made much of the washerwoman.

And yet, the prisoner's motive had looked terribly convincing, and although the nightdress story was not firmly proved it was certainly very suggestive. With such evidence before them, the magistrates would have had no hesitation in sending the case to the Assizes, in order that the responsibility should pass to a jury: they would have had no hesitation, that is, if the prisoner had been a vagrant or one of the village ne'er-do-wells. Only—and this was all the trouble—the prisoner was Miss Constance Kent.

4

It was while the minds of the magistrates were in that state of uncertainty that the defending counsel rose to address the Court.

He must certainly have sized up the embarrassment of the magistrates very accurately.

'I think,' he said, 'the duty which I have to perform here today in this most important case is an exceedingly clear and simple one, and I think, gentlemen, that the duty devolving on you is not less clear. My duty is to ask that this young lady be instantly liberated and restored to her friends—and I apprehend that it will be, as I have said, not only your duty but your pleasure to say "aye" to that at once.

'There is not one tittle of evidence against this young lady—not one word upon which a finger can be laid to show that she is guilty, nor can the finger of infamy in respect to this matter be pointed against her. I ask you to consider the effect of dragging this young lady from home at such a time, if she is really innocent, as I believe she is. I know that an atrocious murder has been committed, but I am afraid that it has been followed by a judicial murder of a scarcely less atrocious character. . . . It will never, never be forgotten that this young lady was dragged from her house and sent like a common felon, a common vagrant, to Devizes gaol. I say, therefore, that this step ought to have been taken only after the most mature consideration, and after something like tangible evidence, and not upon the fact that a paltry bed-gown was missing. . . .

'I say that to drag this young lady from her home in such a way and at such a time, when her heart was already harrowed by the death of her dear little brother, and when, more than at any other time, she needed the affectionate sympathy of her family, is quite sufficient to excite in her favour the sympathy of every man in this county, and not only that, but that of every man of unbiassed mind in this land. . . . The steps you have taken will be such as to ruin her life. Her prospects are already blighted. Every hope is gone with regard to this young girl. If she is innocent, as I believe, it is really terrible to contemplate the result to her, and it must be particularly so to gentlemen of feeling like yourselves.'

Counsel had, of course, a great deal more to say. He proceeded to tear the evidence to shreds. . . . 'The sole fact—and I am ashamed in this land of liberty and justice to refer to it—is the suspicion of Mr. Whicher, a man eager in pursuit of the murderer, and anxious for the reward which has been offered,[1] and it is upon his suspicion, unsupported by the slightest evidence whatever, that this step has been taken.' Counsel spoke also of the meanness—'I say the ineffable meanness, I may say the discredit, and I was about to say the disgrace'—of Inspector Whicher's handling of the case. And he concluded: 'The first step in this case' (i.e. Constance Kent's arrest, on the magistrates' warrant) 'it would be difficult to justify. Let me ask you to pause before you follow it

[1] £100 by the Government and £100 by Mr. Kent.

up by another which would be still more unjustifiable and may expose you to the grave accusation of having very far exceeded the duties devolving upon you. . . . It would, indeed, astonish any judge to be told, on reading the examination taken last Friday and today, that this young lady had been, thereupon, sent to gaol charged with having murdered her brother. . . . I call upon you in the interests not of humanity only, but of clear and simple justice, to detain her not one moment longer in custody, but to liberate her, and restore her to that home from which she ought never to have been taken.'

5

When the magistrates retired, it took them only a quarter of an hour to make up their minds. Or, more exactly perhaps, to devise a way by which they could avoid making up their minds—they must have wanted very much to avoid 'grave accusation' by an astonished judge, as well as the accusation of their own feelings, but equally to avoid the release of a prisoner who might possibly be guilty. So the Chairman announced that he and those with him were not satisfied that the prisoner was innocent of the crime with which she was charged; on the other hand, neither were they satisfied that she was guilty. They did not feel justified in setting her entirely free; but neither did they feel justified, in view of her youth and, ah—that is, her youth, in condemning her to the further period in gaol which would result from her being committed for trial. The evidence which had been brought before them was insufficient for a committal. If she were indeed guilty, further evidence might later be produced. In view of that possibility, they had decided to discharge her in recognizances of £200 to come up if called upon. When those recognizances were entered, she would be free to leave the Court.

6

We read in *The Western Daily Press* of August 2nd, 1860: 'On Friday evening, when Miss Constance Kent returned to her home after her incarceration in Devizes Gaol, the scene which ensued between her and the members of her family was of the most painful description. Her sisters and parents clasped her in the most passionate and exciting manner, embracing her most tenderly, and the sobbing and weeping and embraces were continued for a considerable time. At length, however, it subsided, and since then the young lady has presented a very subdued and contemplative demeanour.'

7

Inspector Jonathan Whicher and Sergeant Frederick Williamson travelled back to London. The 'Prince of Detectives' had failed in what might have been his greatest case. For, in spite of those 'recognizances to come up if called upon', Constance Kent had, in effect, been found Not Guilty and discharged. Everyone took that to be the meaning of the verdict.

There were leading articles in the Press on it.

Generally, the line the papers took was that the Metropolitan Police had come very near to causing a miscarriage of justice. Ever since the Force was created, there had been popular fear, shown in numerous printed broadcasts and in the newspapers, that 'Peel's Bloody Gang' would misuse their power and oppress innocent people. It was now said that that was exactly what had happened. The words of the defence counsel at the trial were widely quoted—particularly the passages about 'dragging this young lady from her home and sending her like a common felon to gaol' and 'the disgrace of Inspector Whicher's handling of the case'.

It was no ordinary case, because it had aroused so much popular attention; and the vituperation which followed its conclusion was couched in no ordinary language. As *The Annual Register* for the year 1860 declared: 'The grounds on which this accusation was made were so frivolous, and the evidence by which it was attempted to be supported so childish, that the proceedings can only be described as absurd and cruel.'

Sir Richard Mayne must have writhed in his office chair as he read those words.

The Metropolitan Police had only been in existence for thirty-one years, and was still regarded in some quarters as an experiment. It was not yet sufficiently well established to withstand any widespread unpopularity and hostile criticism. If that criticism led to a general outcry against it, there might even be a move for its disbandment.

Very earnestly, Sir Richard must have hoped that the newspapers would soon become interested in something else, so that the criticism would be dropped; and also that the Detective Department would not create more trouble —and further danger—by making more mistakes.

PART TWO

Sequel to The First Crisis

CHAPTER 5

Crime in London

1

Sir Richard Mayne was by no means the only man at Great Scotland Yard whose mind was disturbed by the outcome of that case.

Inspector Whicher, of course, took it very hardly. He was young enough to have a great career in front of him. Within a year or two, as everyone knew, Inspector Thornton was due to retire, and then Whicher, with an unbroken record of success behind him, would have been the senior officer of the Detective Department, and in all probability its first undisputed Head, without an equal or a rival.

But it looked extremely doubtful if he would ever be in that position, now, with Sir Richard feeling as he did . . . with Sir Richard, moreover, quite obviously planning some new system of organisation.

And, apart from that, Whicher must have had personal feelings of chagrin, made all the worse because he remained convinced that he had not made any mistake at all. . . .

Then, there was Sergeant Williamson, who also took it hardly. For several years, Jonathan Whicher had been his leader, his instructor, his friend—and, in fact, his idol. Being trained by Inspector Whicher had always made the fulfilment of the ambition seem more certain. Knowing Whicher so well, and getting a little reflected glory from his repeated successes, had been among the joys of life.

It was impossible to read those scathing references to Whicher—to see the terms 'meanness', 'discredit' and 'disgrace' applied to him—without burning indignation. And as for the future—— Some men would have thought—perhaps some men in the Detective Department did think—that if the Inspector was now discredited in the eyes of Sir Richard, that would lead to quicker promotion for the better men in the junior ranks. But Frederick Williamson would never have had any such thought. The keynote of his character, as became extremely evident during the remaining years of his life, was a sense of loyalty and friendship. He would have felt nothing but indignation and sorrow that Whicher should be held in less esteem.

There is, indeed, some evidence[1] that that was the moment when Frederick Williamson put away the last remnants of frivolity and became aware that life was a grim business. Till then, for all his ambitious interest in work, he had enjoyed the 'barneys' and had been a leader in them. The more riotous or hilarious they were, the better. But now . . . He found himself on a committee, with Tim Cavanagh and Eccles, to organise a farewell party for a police-inspector who was retiring. The inspector was long-winded and spoke in reply to the toast for thirty minutes. Eccles then threw a peeled orange and hit the inspector on the nose, after which speech-making ended and everyone had a good time. But Williamson, who

[1] On the authority of Chief-Inspector Cavanagh.

would once have found all that extremely amusing, now saw nothing at all funny in it and became bored if not actually sulky. When called upon for the usual song, he refused to sing.

Clearly, he was taking a very different view of life from the one he had held before the disastrous events in Somerset.

2

Sir Richard Mayne was determined that mistakes which brought discredit on the Metropolitan Police should not occur again. For one thing, no officer should henceforth be allowed to go off on a case and act entirely on his own responsibility. The work of the Detective Department, like that of all the other departments, would have to be closely supervised.

But before changes in organisation could be made to make that the general practice, another important case was on hand. A seventy-year-old widow was murdered in Stepney on August 14th, 1860, less than a fortnight after the end of the case in Somerset.

It was, indeed, a most remarkable case. In the words of *The Annual Register*: 'The Stepney murder will remain memorable in the annals of crime, for it was attended by a combination of circumstances which read more like the complicated guilt of a French novel, or an Adelphi drama, than a possible occurrence in real life.'

Naturally, at that moment, it could not possibly be entrusted to Inspector Whicher. Sir Richard therefore put Inspector Thornton in charge of it.

It may be assumed that just then Inspector Thornton had a great deal of work on his hands, including several cases which would normally have gone to Whicher. He therefore decided—though it is quite possible that Sir Richard Mayne encouraged him, or ordered him, to do so, as part of the new system—to employ Sergeant Thomas on the case: the sergeant was to do the work, while the Inspector directed matters and held the responsibility. But in fact, for reasons quite apart from any organisations new or old, the important part of the case was handled by Sergeant Tanner.

The widow, Mrs. Emsley, was wealthy: she was reputed to have an income of £5,000 a year, obtained from rents on property which she owned. She was cantankerous, secretive and parsimonious, and she liked to keep a close eye on her money. Consequently she went from door to door collecting the rents herself, although for the more distant areas she employed 'unofficial agents'. One of her agents was a cobbler, a certain Mr. Emm.

Mrs. Emsley didn't believe in wasting much money over repairs to her property. She always bought materials for the work at bargain prices, and she had the repairs done by men who would work 'after hours' at cheap rates. One of those men was a plasterer, a certain Mr. George Mullins.

Needless to say, Mrs. Emsley's habit of collecting her own rents meant that there was always a good deal of money in her house. Consequently, she never let callers in at her door, without first peering at them, with the door only open an inch or two and the chain up.

It was Mr. Emm who first reported that something was amiss. He went to Mrs. Emsley's solicitor and said that she had not been seen for four days, that he had called several times, with collected rent, and had got no reply to his knocking and ringing. The house was then broken into, and the widow was found dead, with horrible head-wounds caused by a 'blunt instrument'.

The first thing that Sergeant Thomas discovered was that there were no signs of forcible entry. When that was coupled with the stories of Mrs. Emsley's invariable suspicion of callers, it was clear that the murderer would only have got in if she had recognised him and trusted him.

That limited the field of suspects very much; but nevertheless there was no evidence to justify an arrest. There were rumours and suspicions, of course, but they were a different matter. For instance, a sailor named Mitchell came forward and told the police that on the morning after the murder he had seen George Mullins in the street 'with bulky pockets' and in a state of great nervous excitement. There didn't seem to be much in that, but nevertheless Mullins was summoned to Great Scotland Yard and questioned by Inspector Thornton and Sergeant Thomas as to his movements. He had, it seems, no difficulty in satisfying them that he was an innocent man.

A fortnight thus passed, and a reward of £300 was offered for information that would lead to a conviction.

Now, it so happened that Sergeant Tanner had been in the room at Great Scotland Yard when Inspector Thornton put his questions to George Mullins. It also happened that Tanner lived in a house in Stepney, quite close to the scene of the crime. He was there one evening when Mullins called on him, with the explanation that he had some information which might be of value to the police, but that he didn't want to go all the way to Scotland Yard to tell it.

Mullins's story was that he had been doing a little detective work on his own. That kind of thing came naturally to him, he explained, because he had formerly been a police-sergeant and was now retired on a pension.

Having known poor Mrs. Emsley quite well, he was naturally interested in the case, and it seemed to him that the person most likely to have murdered her was Mr. Emm. With that idea in his mind, he had been posing as a herb-picker in the fields outside Emm's cottage and keeping a watch. At 5 o'clock on the previous morning, he had seen Emm creep into a ruined building and come out carrying a large parcel which he took into his house. A few minutes later, Emm had reappeared with a smaller parcel which he took to a shed beside the cottage, coming out again a short time afterwards—very furtively—without any parcel at all. Wasn't it obvious from that, Mullins demanded, that Emm was engaged in hiding the booty which he had stolen at the time of the murder?

At any earlier time, Sergeant Tanner would probably have followed up this clue immediately, even although it wasn't directly one of his own cases. But everyone at Great Scotland Yard knew how the Commissioner was now feeling about 'independent action', and the new rules which were being made. Tanner therefore said cautiously that he would report the matter to Inspector Thornton. Mullins raised no objection to that: but there was, of course, that offer of a £300 reward, and he did not want Sergeant Tanner to think it convenient to 'forget' where the information had come from. He therefore said, 'Do not act without me, and I will see you all right.' Later, to make the point still clearer, he said, 'If this goes off all right, I will take care of you.'

The next morning, Inpector Thornton, Sergeant Tanner and Sergeant Thomas took a cab from Great Scotland Yard to Emm's cottage, stopping on the way to pick up George Mullins. The Inspector told Mullins to keep out of sight. Mullins grumbled at that, but the Inspector explained that he did not want Emm, at that stage, to know where the information had come from; and as that amounted to official acknowledgement that the reward would be his, Mullins was satisfied.

Sergeant Tanner then searched the cottage. He found nothing to arouse suspicions, and came out and told the Inspector. The search was then about to be called off, but Mullins pressed forward and said it was no use looking in the cottage, because he had seen Emm take the parcel into the adjoining shed: the place to look, he declared, was behind a stone slab in that shed.

The search was then renewed. There *was* a stone slab in the shed, and behind it Sergeant Thomas found a paper parcel tied with part of an apron-string. Inside the outer wrapping was a smaller parcel tied with the waxed thread used by cobblers: and in that were four spoons and a cheque for £10, payable as rent to Mrs. Emsley.

George Mullins was plainly delighted at the discovery, and still more delighted when Emm was arrested. But he was considerably less delighted when Inspector Thornton said, 'We want you too, George Mullins.'

Unfortunately for himself, however, he had nothing more effective to say than, 'What? After giving you the information?' He had no explanation to give of how he could have seen, from his position as a herb-picker in the fields, that the parcel had been hidden *behind a stone slab* inside the shed!

After his arrest, part of an apron string, corresponding to the piece used for tying up the outer parcel, was found in his cottage; and a lump of cobblers' wax, such as Mr. Emm, a shoemaker, would have used if it had been he who handled the string on the inner parcel, was found on his mantelpiece. A plasterer's hammer belonging to him was found to fit some of the wounds on Mrs. Emsley's head. And it was discovered that he had recently flung into the dustbin a boot which exactly fitted into a footprint on a bloodstained floorboard in Mrs. Emsley's house.

So, on November 19th, 1860, after Mr. Emm had been released, George Mullins was executed for the murder of Mrs. Emsley. He would probably not have been hanged, or even seriously suspected, if he had not been too anxious to add £300 to his gains and to make himself additionally secure by getting a scapegoat for his crime.

3

The number of men in the Detective Department had by then increased to sixteen, which made it easier for Sir Richard Mayne to establish his new system. Henceforth, no one in the Detective Department was ever to act 'on his own'; the work of sergeants was to be overseen by inspectors, the work of the inspectors was to be controlled by the Commissioner himself. Sir Richard must have felt that that made things perfectly safe. . . .

There is no record of why, in 1861, a case of murder at Kingswood in Surrey, which was outside the Metropolitan area, was handled by the Detective Department—or of why it was entrusted to Inspector Whicher. Perhaps the case was regarded as particularly important because the murder occurred in a Rectory. Perhaps the idea was to give Jonathan Whicher one more chance. Perhaps it was felt that under the new system even Whicher couldn't go wrong.

On June 9th, the Rector of Kingswood was away from home, and Mrs. Halliday, the wife of his parish clerk, was sleeping alone at the Rectory as caretaker. During the night, two men broke in by way of her bedroom window. They dragged her out of bed, tied her with cord and gagged her. . . . But they were not very skilful at the gagging, and she died of suffocation.

The thieves then took fright and fled. They did not stay to take any loot. And yet it is just possible that one of them was sufficiently cool to adopt one form of protection.

Under the bed, within a few inches of the dead body, was found a pocket-book. In it were various papers, including a 'certificate of employment' in the name, and with a description, of a German called Johann Carl Franz. There was also the last sheet of a letter, in German, from a well-known opera-singer.

It was Sergeant Robinson, acting under Inspector Whicher, who found the papers. They seemed to make the case perfectly clear; and it became all the more so when Sergeant Robinson discovered that, on the day before the crime, two Germans had bought in Reigate a ball of cord of a very unusual make, and that it was that type of cord which had been used for securing Mrs. Halliday.

There was, obviously, nothing more to be done except to start a hue and cry throughout the country for a German with the name of Johann Carl Franz and answering to the description in the papers which had been left behind.

Within a few days, a destitute German was arrested as a vagrant in London, and it was found that his appearance tallied with that in the description. He denied at first that he was Franz, but later he admitted that. He was then charged with the murder.

Inspector Whicher must have been quite sure that no mistake had been made that time. A personal description of the murderer was infinitely better evidence than a mere missing nightgown.

But Franz had a story to tell.

He said he had come to England with two German companions, one of whom bore the name of Adolphe Krohn. They had quarrelled with him and left him: he had been asleep when they went, and when he awoke, he found that they had stolen his pocket-book. What money he had, he said, had been in the pocket-book, and without the 'certificate of employment' he had been unable to get work. So he had soon become destitute. Then he had heard of the murder, and had learnt that there was a hue and cry for somebody with his own name. Naturally, therefore, as he explained, he had denied his name when arrested.

It was, of course, an extremely improbable story. It was just the tale that any murderer who had left incriminating papers on the scene of the crime would have to tell—it was the only one he could put up, to escape the gallows. He had no alibi, and he couldn't produce the two Germans. There wasn't any reason to suppose that Adolphe Krohn and the other man had ever existed.

The case against him therefore proceeded rapidly, and it looked very much as if Jonathan Wicher's name as 'the Prince of Detectives' would be restored: even if there was nothing very remarkable, here, in the way of detection, it would at least be a success which would do something to wipe out the memory of a failure.

And then—— The opera singer appeared. She had never heard of Johann Carl Franz, the prisoner in the dock. Her letter, the one found in the pocket-book, had been written to another German, a man named Adolphe Krohn.

With that much of confirmation of Franz's story before them the jury refused to convict him. He was found 'Not Guilty' and discharged.

So Inspector Whicher had failed again. This time, of course, there could have been excuses for him. Not only he, but everyone else concerned in the case, had been certain up to that last minute of the prisoner's guilt, and nobody could have foreseen the sudden change in the weight of evidence. But, of course, nobody—except perhaps Sergeant Frederick Williamson—bothered to make the excuses. Jonathan Whicher was finished. He had lost all his old powers. He could only make mistakes now. He would never be any good again.

4

A book of this sort must inevitably give the impression—which in any case is held by all readers of modern detective-novels—that detectives are only employed on 'big' cases, and that they have no routine work of dealing with the comparatively minor daily—and nightly—crimes of a big city. That is certainly not so, and it was particularly far from being the case a century ago. The following account of life in the streets of London[1] is included here to show how the members of the Detective Department and the constables of the Metropolitan Police (now risen in numbers to about 6,000) were kept employed.

'This great metropolis, ever awake in the constant movement of its population, with streets so wide and so well lighted, and guarded by the best-arranged system

[1] From *The Annual Register*, 1862.

of police known to any capital, has been held during a great part of this year in a state of chronic terror by a gang of ruffians. . . . They use a method of highway plunder which consists in one ruffian seizing an unsuspecting traveller by the neck and crushing in his throat, while another simultaneously rifles his pockets; the scoundrels then decamp, leaving their victim on the ground, writhing in agony, with tongue protruding and eyes starting from their sockets, unabled to give an alarm or attempt pursuit. . . .

'These savage Thugs committed their crimes in the most public places and frequently in broad day. These cruel acts were committed in such places as Lincoln's Inn Fields, Brunswick Square, Long Acre, Bloomsbury Street, Pall Mall, Cockspur Street, and others of the most frequented thoroughfares of the metropolis. . . .

'These dreadful outrages spread terror over all the millions that inhabit London.

'With the long evenings and dark nights, the evil and its terror rose to the height; the police force was largely increased, and it was evident that a systematic war must be waged against the criminal class that furnished these wretches. . . .

'In all, about twenty-four of the most dangerous ruffians that had held London in subjection were brought to justice. . . . The sentences were all such as would be felt by their confederates—penal servitude for life, for 20, 15, or 10 years. . . .

'The reign of terror was at an end, and the inhabitants of the metropolis once more traversed their streets without starting at every footstep or turning pale at every shadow.'

5

When Inspector Thornton was due to retire, Sergeant Frederick Williamson had a brief interview with Sir Richard Mayne, and emerged as an inspector. He was then only 32.

It was a big step forward towards the achievement of his ambition, but he found himself shouldering an enormous responsibility. For Inspector Whicher was by that time a very sick man, and even if a fair proportion of the duties had been allotted to him, he would not have been able to perform them. The doctors of today would have had no doubt that his illness was brought on by worry.

Williamson did not even have Inspector Richardson, the inspector from the Executive Department of the Commissioner's office, who had frequently lent a hand in detective cases, to help him, for Richardson had retired at the same time as Thornton, and had been succeeded by Inspector Searle, who had not had the same experience.

Thus Williamson had in effect to bear the whole burden of the Department, on the strength of what he had learnt during about ten years as a sergeant. It was not an easy task: and it certainly cannot have been made easier by the fact that Jonathan Whicher still sat in the Inspectors' Room at Great Scotland Yard, even if he could do very little work. It is never a comfortable position to work under the eyes of your instructor, when you have become nominally that instructor's equal; and it is particularly embarrassing when the instructor is suffering from an acute nervous breakdown and something approaching melancholia.

Once, during those unhappy days, a most astonishing thing happened: a rumour reached Williamson's ears that Constance Kent had confessed, to one of her relatives, that she was guilty after all.

It is a matter of history that that happened, and that nothing was done about it: 'they found it unadvisable,' says one of the records, 'to act upon the fresh information which had reached them.' May we not imagine, however, a little more than that?

Joyfully, Frederick Williamson would have taken the good news to Whicher. For more than a minute, Whicher would not have answered. Then . . . 'Thankee, Mr. Williamson. Thankee, my boy. But it would not be any use. No use at all. Do more harm than good, maybe, to follow up a thing like that.'

'But, sir'—though he was now technically Whicher's equal in rank, Williamson would never have lost the habit of saying 'sir' to his old chief—'But, sir, it will do everything for you. You'll get back—— Everyone will know you were right.'

Whicher would slowly have shaken his head. 'It might not go that way. Besides, it doesn't matter about me. I'm finished. Had my day, you know. Shan't last much longer.'

It wouldn't have been in Williamson's character to leave things there: he was always faithful to his friends. But if he went to Sir Richard Mayne, asking to be allowed to re-open the case, the Commissioner would have been short and sharp with him. 'Oh no, Inspector Williamson. Not on any account. There cannot be anything in that rumour of a confession. It is quite obvious that Miss Kent was not guilty. Accusing her was merely a blunder, and arresting her a worse one.'

That would have been all. 'They' found it inadvisable to act. . . .

6

When at last Jonathan Whicher retired, a broken man with his health completely wrecked, Richard Tanner joined Williamson in the Inspectors' Room.

As far as experience went, he was a poor substitute for Whicher, having had only eight years in the Detective Department, and having spent part of that time on clerical work. He was, however, a young man of energy and initiative. He very soon had an opportunity to show both of those qualities.

In the words of *The Times* of July 11th, 1864: 'One of the most atrocious crimes that ever disgraced this country was perpetrated late on Saturday evening in a first-class carriage of a passenger train on the North London Railway, when a gentleman, Mr. Thomas Briggs . . . was murderously assailed, plundered, and thrown out of the train.'

The first discovery was made when the train stopped at Hackney and two bank clerks entered the compartment, no doubt thinking themselves lucky to have secured an empty one. The compartment, however, was not completely empty: it contained a walking-stick, a black beaver hat, and a small black bag. The two bank clerks must have been looking with surprise at these articles (which, like the appurtenances of the Invisible Man, seemed to indicate the presence of someone who wasn't there), when one of them rested his hand on one of the seat-cushions and found it to be covered with something wet, sticky and red. . . .

About ten minutes later, the driver of another train

saw 'a dark object' lying at the side of the rails between Hackney Wick and Bow. He stopped his train, got down, and found the body of a man—a man who was alive but unconscious, and who died twenty-four hours later, without having been able to speak.

Papers on the body led quickly to identification by Mr. Briggs' son. It appeared that a pair of gold eyeglasses and a gold watch and chain were missing, which seemed to make it clear that robbery had been the object of the assault. And then came the dramatic discovery—and, for that matter, the very far-reaching discovery—that while the black bag and the stick had been carried by Mr. Briggs that night, the black beaver hat *was not his*.

He had been wearing a 'silk hat, Paris nap of the best quality, with a white silk lining'—and of that there was no sign at all.

Superintendent Howie and Inspector Kerrissey of K Division of the Metropolitan Police were in charge of the case, but Sir Richard Mayne appointed 'Inspector Tanner of the Detective Department' to assist them: and Tanner took Sergeant George Clarke with him. Sir Richard appears to have made it clear to everyone concerned that he wasn't going to trust his youngest and least-experienced inspector very far, and that everything was to be done very closely under his own supervision. Indeed, it is this case which produced a further step in Sir Richard's new system—a development which has survived to the present day, in the writing by detectives of frequent reports to their superior officers.

'A very lengthy report from the officers in charge of the case was sent in to Sir Richard Mayne late last night.'

'The excitement created by the murder is growing daily

more and more intense. . . . Inspector Kerrissey made a report on the subject to Sir Richard Mayne.'[1]

This time, there was to be no arrest of an innocent person, through the impetuous action of a junior officer acting 'on his own responsibility'!

The curious business of the two hats seemed to have only one possible explanation, even if it was an almost incredible one: this must have been an unpremeditated crime, the assailant having intended to do no more than stun his victim for purposes of robbery: then he must have seen that he had hit harder than he meant to do—probably he thought Mr. Briggs to be already dead—and have panicked. He would then have pushed the body through the window, and have jumped out of the train at the next station, accidentally taking with him the victim's hat in place of his own.

Admittedly, there was a great difference between a hard silk hat and a soft beaver one—a difference which would leap to the touch of the fingers if not, for some reason, to the eye. But it was just possible that such a mistake could be made, if the panic was sufficiently strong: anyway, it *had* been made, and there was additional evidence of panic in the fact that the murderer had snatched up the eye-glasses and the watch but had overlooked £4. 10s. in cash, which Mr. Briggs had had in his pocket.

The beaver hat had inside it the name of its maker, at a shop in Marylebone, but nevertheless it proved untraceable, as those hats had been sold by the hundred and there was nothing to distinguish one from another. There therefore seemed to be no obvious clue to the murderer, and matters were at a standstill. . . . 'Although the investigations of Inspector Tanner and his corps of detectives

[1] *The Times*, July 13th and 14th, 1864.

were carried on with great perseverance during the whole of yesterday, still up to a late hour last night the murderer had not been captured. . . . The police seem to feel that after their many failures of late years the present case puts them on their trial.'[1]

In the absence of any clue, Inspector Tanner had to use his head in the matter of detection. The murderer, it was argued, was not a professional footpad—if he had been, he would have waylaid someone in the streets and not a fellow-traveller in a railway carriage.[2] The crime was unpremeditated, and the murderer was moved to desperate action by the sight of a gold watch-chain hanging across a waistcoat: therefore he was hard-up and probably hungry. Immediately after the crime, he had been panic-stricken: but panic quietens down in time, whereas hunger only increases in time. By now, therefore, hunger would be in command of the man—and no man would remain hungry while he had in his possession a pair of gold eye-glasses and a gold watch and chain. It would, however, be madness for him to attempt to sell them, at any rate until the hunt had died down. Hunger would press him, while the remains of the panic would restrain him: he would therefore have tried to turn some of his booty into money, though he would have done it in some artful way intended to avoid suspicion.

That reasoning, as it turned out, was exactly correct.

Enquiries at jewellers for someone who had tried to sell a gold watch and chain (or even a pair of eye-glasses) led nowhere. But when Inspector Tanner and Sergeant Clarke started enquiring on the lines of the Inspector's new argument, they found a jeweller in Cheapside who

[1] *The Times*, July 15th, 1864.

[2] This was, in fact, the first murder ever committed on a railway in Britain.

remembered that a man had come into his shop the other day with a gold chain—only he hadn't wanted to sell it, he had only asked to *exchange* it for an inferior chain and a ring. The jeweller had not hesitated to do that, since it wasn't a thing that any dishonest man would want to do. . . . Yet if this was Mr. Briggs' murderer, he had very artfully got possession of articles of jewellery which were not on the official lists of stolen property, and which he could therefore sell without arousing suspicion.

The jeweller's customer was described as a foreigner, probably a German, thin, sallow-faced and hungry-looking. The hunt for such a man was up.

There was not, however, very much to go on, London being full of thin, hungry-looking people, and there being no dearth of foreigners. So again the trail went cold, and Inspector Tanner had to think again.

He had had, he realised, one enormous piece of good fortune—or, to be more exact, something which might possibly prove to be good fortune. The Cheapside jeweller had packed up the ring and chain in one of his own boxes, with his name printed on it—and it was an unusual and striking name, DEATH. A name that anyone would notice. There would be hundreds of boxes with 'Brown' or 'Jones' on them, and nobody would pay any attention: but a box with DEATH printed on it would be sure to attract notice.

A description of the jeweller's box was therefore issued to the Press, and a reward of £300 was offered for 'information leading to the arrest of the criminal'.

7

Three days afterwards, very late in the evening, a cab stopped outside the police station at Paddington Green, and the cabman, a man named Matthews, climbed down from the box and went inside. He was seen by Inspector Steer, the officer on night duty.

Matthews was illiterate and a little long-winded, but the upshot of his story was that for the past two years he had known a German named Franz Muller, who had been working for his brother-in-law. There had been quite a friendship between Matthews and Muller, with Muller coming to dinner two or three times a month—and in fact he had at one time been 'smitten on' Matthews' eldest daughter, but that had been broken off because he had been the jealous kind, and violent at that, always making trouble when other men were around. In spite of that difficulty in the family, the friendship had lasted, so that when, having lost his job, Muller decided to sail for America, he naturally came to say goodbye to Matthews. By way of a parting gift, he then gave a little box to Matthews' younger daughter, aged ten. The little girl played with the box, without anybody paying much attention to it, until one day when Matthews trod on it, and picked it up, and noticed that it had the word 'Death' printed on it, which, in Matthews' opinion, wasn't very nice and, on a child's plaything, wasn't particularly cheerful. . . . Now Mr. Matthews had heard that the police were wanting to get hold of a box with that on it, so here it was, and wasn't there something said about a reward?

Inspector Steer 'at once saw the necessity of immediate action and ordered Matthews to drive him to the house of Mr. Superintendent Tiddy in Marylebone'.[1] By that time, it was very late at night. By the time the long story had been repeated to Superintendent Tiddy, and Matthews had been cross-examined about details, it was past

[1] *The Times*, July 19th, 1864.

midnight. Nevertheless this was such an important matter that the Superintendent decided that his duty was clear: he must put the whole thing at once before Sir Richard Mayne himself. So he and the Inspector got into the cab and Matthews (who was doubtless becoming quite excited by this time about the prospect of that £300 reward) drove them to Sir Richard's house at 83, Chester Square, Pimlico.

Sir Richard, we must infer, felt that that was really going a little too far. It was all very correct for things to be done under his supervision, but really, at 1.0 in the morning, and when he had had a long and tiring day! At any rate, he was very curt about it and 'instructed the police officials to communicate at once with Inspector Tanner'.

So the cab, with the Superintendent and the Inspector, had to drive all the way to Stepney. By that time, some confusion seems to have crept into the information so that a doubt arose as to whether Muller had already sailed for America, or whether he was only in the 'packing up' stage—or whether it was all a bluff. So the cab, now with Inspector Tanner as well as Superintendent Howie, Superintendent Tiddy and Inspector Steer in it, waited outside Matthews' house for the rest of the night. It was not until 5 a.m. that the officers finally decided that it wasn't a bluff and they were wasting their time.

Inspector Tanner didn't waste any time during the rest of the day, however. In particular, he obtained a lot more evidence from Matthews.

Some time before, during Muller's more prosperous days, he had admired a hat—a black beaver hat—worn by his friend the cabman, and had asked for one like it to be bought for him. From certain distinctive marks, Matthews was able to identify the hat found in the railway carriage after the murder as the one he had himself bought for Muller.

Matthews also had a photograph of Muller, and from this Muller was identified by Mr. Death, the jeweller in Cheapside, as the man who had exchanged the gold chain two days after the murder. And finally, it was found that Muller had pawned the inferior chain which he had obtained from Mr. Death, and had obtained other small sums of money as well, and had then booked a passage to America in the *Victoria*, which was sailing from London docks.

8

The *Victoria* was a sailing-ship and was not due to reach New York for five or six weeks. If Muller was to be caught, someone had to cross the Atlantic more quickly than that, in order to obtain an extradition order and arrest the murderer before he could disappear in the United States. There was only one way in which that could be done: the Home Secretary applied to the Admiralty, and Inspector Tanner sailed in the 'Admiralty steamer' *The City of Manchester*. With him were Sergeant Clarke, Mr. Matthews and Mr. Death, both of whom were needed for the extradition proceedings. In another steamship, *The City of Cork*, went Inspector Kerrissey.

For six weeks, the progress of that extraordinary chase across the Atlantic was reported in the newspapers, the captains of all ships that entered British ports being interviewed and asked when and where they had sighted any of the three ships. Steam was racing against sail, the new invention against the old.

Steam won the race. Muller was arrested before he

could go ashore in America. Among his possessions was found a silk hat ('Paris nap of the best quality') of unusual design: on examination it was found that the crown had been cut down by an inch and a half (the piece cut out being the part on which Mr. Briggs had written his name), the edges then being sewn and pasted together.[1]

Among the many items of interest reported by the Press concerning the last stages of the case is the news that while being escorted back to England, Muller passed the time tranquilly and read Dickens' novels. He was mobbed at Euston Station (where the triumphant Inspector Tanner and Sergeant Clarke were met and greeted by Inspector Williamson and Sergeant Thomas) and again at Bow Street. It is said that a crowd of 20,000 people watched his execution on November 14th, 1864.

[1] Silk hats of less than the usual height were afterwards put on the market under the name of 'Muller cut-downs'. It is said that from them originated Bowler hats.

CHAPTER 6

Training a Detective

1

It was essential to Sir Richard Mayne's new system that two detectives should henceforth be employed on every case, the senior of the two being directly responsible to himself. In effect, since there were still only two inspectors, that meant that (as in Whicher's case at Kingswood Rectory) a sergeant did most of the work, while an inspector kept a close eye on him—a particularly close eye because (again as in the case at Kingswood) it was the inspector who was held responsible if anything went wrong.

That method of working out the system had additional advantages: it gave the sergeants a practical training, under strict supervision, and it also showed clearly which were the best of the sergeants. By 1865, Sergeant George Clarke (who had been with Inspector Tanner to America in pursuit of Muller) was at last coming to the fore. A comparatively new recruit, Sergeant James J. Thomson, was making his mark. Two other men who are to figure prominently in the later passages of our chronicle—Nathaniel Druscovich (another new recruit) and William

Palmer—together with an Irishman named Mulvaney and a man who was rather older than most of the sergeants—John Shore—were definitely marked out for promotion.

2

Frederick Williamson had had his training from Jonathan Whicher, and no doubt Whicher, with his vast experience and complete self-confidence, felt no embarrassment about acting as a teacher. He would have said, 'I wouldn't have done it that way, my boy: this is what I would have done', and no young sergeant would have dreamt of questioning his wisdom.

But when Williamson, in his turn, was called upon to give the instruction, the position was very different: his experience was still, comparatively, very limited—he was a young man—and no one was inclined to take him as a pontifical authority.

Nevertheless, he had qualities which stood him in good stead. He has been described as 'hardworking, persevering, obstinate and courageous': which is just another way of saying that when he had made up his mind to do a thing, he did it. It has also been said of him that he always had his own opinion and was never afraid to express it:[1] which is just another way of saying that he was completely self-confident. In addition, he 'was kind-hearted to a fault' and he always inspired confidence even in the most timid of his pupils.

And training younger men was one of his duties which he always liked.

So it is safe to say that he would have been an exceptionally good instructor.

[1] Lansdowne.

3

By that time—inspired, perhaps, by the knowledge of French which he had gained from the tutor in Leicester Square while the other young sergeants were at the theatres—Williamson was taking special interest in the subject of extradition. Too often, a criminal would slip through the net and vanish on the other side of either the English Channel or the Atlantic Ocean, and it was essential to have a working arrangement with both the men at the Sureté and the police of America, so as to have the criminals promptly brought back.

Probably it was this work which made Williamson inclined to take a special interest in the two men under him who had a knowledge of Continental languages: James J. Thomson and Nat. Druscovich. He was always careful to employ one or other of them as his sergeant in cases which might involve negotiations with the Paris Sureté.

One such case came to hand in 1865. Williamson then sent for Sergeant Druscovich, an Englishman of Polish extraction. Druscovich had, as a matter of fact, a distinctly foreign look about him—in those days it would probably have been called 'Frenchy'—which was enhanced by a smart Imperial beard and more suave manners than were common amongst most Englishmen of the day.

This particular case was hardly a matter for the Yard at all, since it did not refer to any crime committed in England: but the officials of the Sureté needed help, and Williamson was anxious about the principle of *quid pro quo*.

A Bordeaux wine-merchant named Vital Douat had recently declared himself a bankrupt—but some of his creditors were suspicious that the bankruptcy was fraudulent, since they alleged that Douat had a lot of money secretly 'put by'. Whether that was true or not—and it almost certainly is true that Douat would have regarded such a bankruptcy as an excellent trick on his creditors—was never legally proved, because the opportunity for proving it never arose. Before the bankruptcy question could be dealt with, Douat's wife presented herself at the offices of a French insurance company with the sad news that her husband was dead . . . and a claim on life insurance to the value of 125,000 francs.[1]

The insurance policy was a new one, on which only a single premium had been paid. Not unnaturally, insurance companies are never very happy about claims in those circumstances. This one was well supported: Madame Douat had brought with her a medical certificate of the cause of death, the registration of the death, and a burial certificate. But perhaps it was just that profusion of documents—more than were either usual or necessary—that aroused suspicion.

In addition to that there was the fact that the Bordeaux wine-merchant had not died at his home in Bordeaux, or even anywhere in France: he had died, and been buried, in Plaistow, in the East End of London.

The insurance company had therefore suspected fraud and had placed the matter in the hands of the Sureté. And the Sureté had consulted Scotland Yard, asking either for an assurance that the documents were genuine or proof that they were not.

4

Sergeant Druscovich took away the papers and began his enquiries. The certificate of registration of death was

[1] Then about £5,000.

certainly in order, and in view of that there seemed no need to bother about the burial certificate. But the medical certificate, Druscovich found, was rather peculiar. There was nothing specially noteworthy, of course, in the fact that the doctor's signature was illegible—or practically so—but it was certainly surprising that the doctor had omitted his address. . . .

It says something for Inspector Williamson's ideas of discipline that Sergeant Druscovich did not go back to report that, as soon as he discovered it: instead, he carried out the orders that had been given him, to the extent of wasting a day over a fruitless search for a doctor whose name bore any resemblance to that on the certificate—and who had ever had a patient named Vital Douat.

When at last he did report it, Williamson's suspicions were aroused about the whole matter. Did it mean that the origins of the doctor's certificate had been made untraceable—deliberately? If so, was the certificate a fake? And in that case, was Vital Douat still alive, was the insurance claim a complete fraud? And, then, where was Vital Douat now?

Thus it became necessary to regard the case as a much more serious one, in which the main task was not to check certificates but to trace a missing man.

The next discovery was that Douat's name was not in the Passengers' List of the boat in which, according to the French police, he had crossed the Channel. That suggested that he must have travelled under an alias. But as there was no information as to what the alias was, it was now necessary to take on the exhausting task—or rather, for Sergeant Druscovich to take it on—of tracing all the passengers on the boat that Douat was supposed to have crossed on, and of pursuing them to their homes in order to make sure that none of them was the missing man.

That was patiently done. At the end of it, Druscovich reported to Williamson that he had been able to trace all the passengers except one—a Mr. Roberti Bernardi. Mr. Bernardi, it seemed, had taken lodgings in London, telling the landlord that he was a waiter by profession, but that at the moment, instead of working, he was 'looking after a sick friend'. Later, Mr. Bernardi had told the landlord that his friend had died. Immediately after that, he had left his lodgings and disappeared: Druscovich had not been able to find the slightest trace of where he had gone.

But the interesting thing—the most interesting thing—about that story was that the district in which Mr. Bernardi had taken those lodgings directly he reached England was Plaistow—where M. Vital Douat was supposed to have died.

5

One can imagine, surely, how the next part of this interview between the Inspector and his pupil would have gone. . . .

After he had finished his report, Sergeant Druscovich would have said, 'I don't know whether you only want the facts from me, sir, or whether you are expecting a theory.'

Williamson would have smiled, very good-humouredly, at that. He always liked keen young sergeants. 'I like to see a young man work things out on his own. That is what Inspector Whicher used to say to me, when I was being trained. So go ahead, Sergeant Druscovich: tell me your own theory about this case.'

'Well, sir, here is this Mr. Bernardi looking after a sick friend, who can't be traced, and who is now stated to be dead. The thing I am wondering about is when that friend of Mr. Bernardi's died. Supposing he had died on the boat?'

'Did anyone die on that boat? Did you hear of a corpse being carried ashore?'

'I wouldn't have done, sir, if the friend had died the way I think he did. If Bernardi had murdered him, he would have been carried ashore in Bernardi's cabin trunk, with nobody knowing anything about it.'

Inspector Williamson would immediately have put his finger on the fallacy in that. 'Come, come, Sergeant. I was expecting something more intelligent than that. Douat's name wasn't in the Passengers' List, so he cannot have been on board the ship.'

Druscovich would not have been put off by that. 'I know, sir. But—well, supposing Bernardi was one of the creditors in the fraudulent bankruptcy, and he had murdered Douat in France? Then, if he thought it would be easier to dispose of a corpse in England than in his own country, he would only have had to smuggle the body on board ship and then off again——'

'That is quite ridiculous. The Customs Officers——'

Now, Sergeant Druscovich—who wasn't quite English—was a very smart young man: smart in every way, as was proved by certain events in his subsequent career. So he would have smiled at that. He might—if the Inspector wasn't actually looking at him—have winked, even. 'Any experienced traveller, sir, would tell you how to arrange that. The Customs Officers have their price, like everyone else, and they don't look where they are paid not to look. Why, when I came back from Paris last month——'

6

Inspector Williamson did not adopt that theory. He would not have considered for a moment that Sergeant Druscovich's disgraceful suggestion that Customs Officers might be bribed could possibly be true: he would have scorned the idea that they 'have their price, *like everyone else*'.[1]

In any event, it was not his way of dealing with a case to bother himself with speculative theories before he had all the facts in his hands. Sergeant Druscovich was therefore set to trace this Mr. Roberti Bernardi after he left Plaistow: the probability being, as Williamson suggested, that he had gone either into fresh lodgings or to an hotel.

After a long search, trace of him was at last found at an hotel in the Strand, where he had stayed for some days, saying he was a traveller in wines. He was not at the hotel any longer; but he had left behind him some very valuable —if extraordinary—evidence.

Coming to report the discovery to Williamson, Sergeant Druscovich brought with him the waiter from the hotel. . . .

'It's nothing to do with me, sir. I only done what the gentleman asked, by way of a joke, like he said. If there's wrong in it, it wasn't me: I didn't get nothing out of it, not even a tip. . . . Well, sir, this Mr. Bernardi, he's a funny gentleman, quite the joker. And chatty. Not like some of 'em, what scowl at you all through breakfast and growl at you all through dinner. Always cheery, he was, and wanting to take a rise out of people, if there was anyone to take a rise out of, which there wasn't. Well, one day, we was

[1] 'Williamson was a most upright and valuable servant'—Lansdowne. 'He had unswerving integrity and perfect trustworthiness'—Obituary Notice in *The Times*. 'He was a man of the strictest honour'—Sir Edward Clarke.

chatting, him and me, when everyone had finished breakfast and we was alone in the coffee-room. He told me he had a friend who wouldn't ever answer his letters, not however often he wrote to him. He said his friend might as well be dead, for all the answers he got. And he asked me what I'd do, if I had a friend like that, to stir him up. But I didn't know, not having anybody I write letters to except the old woman, when she goes to her Ma, and then it's only to tell her the kids haven't fallen in the fire and I've fed the cat: and she doesn't answer, never. . . .

'Well, sir, this Mr. Bernardi, being a funny gentleman as I told you, said to me a day or two later that saying his friend might as well be dead had given him an idea. He said he was going to send his friend a—a bit of paper telling him he *was* dead, and making it look as if it was written by a doctor.

'He was laughing fit to bust over the joke, and suddenly he takes out a bit of paper and picks up a pen—and then he says, "Tell you what, you write it; my friend won't know your fist, like he does mine."'

Astonishing as that was, the next piece of evidence which Druscovich collected, under Williamson's orders, was equally extraordinary, if not more so.

There was an undertaker in Plaistow who had received a visit from a man who gave his name as Signor Rubini, and who showed him the certificate of the registration of the death of M. Vital Douat and asked him to arrange for the interment. The service was to be conducted at the cemetery by a Roman Catholic priest: there was to be only one coach to follow the hearse, as Signor Rubini was the only mourner.

Signor Rubini, it appeared, had been very much upset throughout the interview, the departed being a very great friend of his, a life-long friend, to whom he had some peculiar tie in the matter of religion. In fact Signor Rubini and poor M. Douat (in spite of the fact that the funeral service was to be conducted in the Roman Church) had belonged to some special religious sect, with peculiar rites. Particularly, Signor Rubini explained to the undertaker, in the matter of death and burial, it being ordained that no hands might touch the body except those of an Elder of the Church. So if the undertaker would kindly deliver a coffin made according to the measurements given him——

7

'Now,' the Inspector may have said to his pupil, 'I suppose you will tell me that Bernardi took all that trouble because he didn't want the undertaker to see the wounds from which Douat died?'

'He wouldn't have done, would he, sir?'

'I suppose not—if he had murdered the man. In fact, to quote Jonathan Whicher again, there is nothing wrong with your theory, Sergeant, except that it isn't right. Though, as a matter of fact, there is, and always has been, one thing about it which is very wrong. You ought to have seen it: I didn't point it out to you, in the hope that you would eventually see it for yourself—you would have learnt more that way. The French police told us that Douat came to England on a certain boat. His name, as you yourself discovered, was not in the Passengers' List. Then how did the police know he was aboard?'

'Oh.' That reasoning would certainly have made young Druscovich hesitate. 'You mean, sir, that they could only have known that, if they had been shadowing him and had actually seen him boarding the ship?'

'Exactly. Or at least very nearly. Perhaps they were not shadowing him and—since they did not arrest him then over the bankruptcy business—it was not one of their own men who saw him. But at least they must have had reliable evidence that he went aboard, so some very trustworthy person—a Customs Officer, possibly—must have supplied it.

'In that case, he was not murdered in France—he was alive on board the boat. But as his name was not in the Passengers' List, he must have been travelling under someone else's name. The only one you failed to check was that of Bernardi. Therefore Bernardi was Douat. And since Bernardi was also, obviously, this Signor Rubini, Douat cannot have been in the coffin. In fact, no one can have been in the coffin: it must have been empty, except possibly for a few stones to give it the correct weight.'

8

In due course, Williamson obtained an exhumation order from the Home Office, and his solution of the problem was proved to be entirely correct. Meanwhile, M. Vital Douat, *alias* Roberti Bernardi, *alias* Rubini, had disappeared once more. Sergeant Druscovich traced him as far as Liverpool, where he had taken ship to America. There was no question of extradition as far as Scotland Yard was concerned, for this was not a British case; and the officials at the Sureté, finding that the claim for the insurance money could not now be pressed, decided to drop the matter.

It was to be hoped, however, that Sergeant Druscovich, at least, had learnt something from the case. And indeed, there is evidence that he took it to heart and remembered it.

For, some years later, when Druscovich was an inspector, the curious case had its sequel. A merchant who had newly arrived in Antwerp took out a large insurance policy on some goods which were waiting on the quay for shipment. The goods were destroyed by fire before they could be loaded—and two barrels of tar were found among the debris. The 'merchant who had newly arrived in Antwerp' (from America, as it happened) learnt of that discovery and decamped to England. There, the search for him was entrusted to Inspector Druscovich. And Druscovich, when he heard the details, said at once, 'Ah, that sounds like a certain M. Vital Douat.'

It was indeed M. Douat. But he was not known as 'Monsieur' when he was serving his term on Devil's Island.

CHAPTER 7

Confession of Guilt

1

It is not very likely that Sir Richard Mayne had any particularly strong sense of drama. He was definitely a realist, and hardly a man of much imagination. Probably, therefore, he only picked on Inspector Williamson, on April 25th, 1865, to go to Bow Street and receive the instructions of Sir Thomas Henry, the Chief Magistrate, because it was Williamson's 'turn' for the next case. But by doing so he created a dramatic situation of great intensity.

When Williamson arrived, he was shown at once into the Chief Magistrate's private room. There, besides Sir Thomas Henry, he found three people: a young woman in black, heavily veiled, a Church of England clergyman, and an elderly woman in the garb of some religious order.

Sir Thomas was talking to the clergyman.[1]

'Did you, in the first instance, induce her to make the confession to you?'

'No, sir. She wished herself to do so.'

[1] There is a contemporary record of Sir Thomas's questions and these answers.

'You did not persuade her?'

'No, sir. She thought of it herself, without my ever suggesting it.'

Sir Thomas then turned to the younger woman, the one in the veil.

'Am I to understand that you have given yourself up of your own free act and will, on this charge?'

Very quietly, and without removing the veil, the young woman said, 'Yes, sir.'

'Anything you say here will be written down and may be used against you. Do you understand that?'

'Yes, sir.'

'Is the paper now produced before me in your own handwriting and written of your own free will?'

'It is, sir.'

2

It is possible that by that point Frederick Williamson had recognised the woman's voice: or, if that was not so, he may have had some faint stirring of memory about it, across the space of the five years since he had heard it in Court. But in any case he was not left long in doubt, for the confession was read aloud:

'I, Constance Emilie Kent, alone and unaided, did, on the night of the 29th June 1860, murder, at Road Hill House, Wiltshire, one Francis Saville Kent. Before the deed, no one knew my intention, nor after my guilt. No one assisted me in the crime, nor in my evasion of discovery.'

3

Frederick Williamson may have been aware, in that moment, that there was tragedy in the fact that a child of sixteen had committed a terrible crime, had been acquitted of it, and now, when twenty-one, was coming, 'of her own free act and will', to end her life in expiation. But probably that aspect of the matter did not impress itself on him very forcibly, for he was accustomed to terrible crimes and their almost inevitable—at any rate, their usual—consequences. What would have forced itself very clearly into his mind at that moment was the other tragedy of the case—that of Jonathan Whicher.

This confession could only mean that Whicher had been right after all. His action of five years ago, which had brought discredit and disgrace upon him; his bringing of 'childish evidence' to support 'a frivolous charge'; his alleged 'meanness' in bringing that charge merely because he wished to secure a monetary reward; all these actions was now shown to have been entirely justified. Jonathan Whicher had not made a mistake—he had been right, through a brilliant act of detection.

During all the last five years, whatever Constance Kent had been doing—hugging her guilty secret and enjoying her escape, presumably—Jonathan Whicher had become more and more discredited, more and more broken, more and more ill and distressed—all because of an alleged mistake which, after all, had not been a mistake. Jonathan Whicher was now dying—whatever the doctors might say of his disease—of a broken heart. His magnificent reputation, his certainty of success in his career, had all been taken from him by that failure which had been a triumph!

4

Williamson would have come out of those reflections with a start as the Chief Magistrate spoke to him.

'You are Inspector Williamson of the Detective Department?'

'Yes, sir.'

'Then I give Miss Kent into your charge. You will take her to Trowbridge. You will take with you this paper, which is her signed confession, and produce it in Court there. She is now in your keeping.'

'Yes, sir.'

Then a cab was fetched, so that Inspector Williamson could take Constance Kent to Paddington Station.[1] The lady in the religious habit (who was the Mother Superior of St. Mary's Home in Brighton) wanted to accompany her and was allowed to do so: though it was not in accordance with the regular procedure, Williamson would not have felt he could be so rigorous as to object, seeing that Sir Thomas had spoken of 'Miss Kent' and not of 'the prisoner'. But although the Mother Superior travelled that day to Trowbridge, it can be assumed that Williamson did not let her have a seat in the compartment in which he had himself locked with the self-confessed murderess.

There is a statement in *The Times* that the long journey from London to Trowbridge was conducted in complete silence: 'Not a single word was spoken during the journey.' That, however, can only be 'intelligent reporting', for Inspector Williamson would not have spoken about it to the Press[2] and Constance Kent would have had no

[1] A full account of this part of the story, with the words used by Sir Thomas Henry, appeared in the contemporary Press.

[2] 'He was by nature very reticent: no outsider could win from him any details of the many "big things" he had put through.' (Arthur Griffiths.)

opportunity to do so. And in fact, it might well be described, rather, as '*un*intelligent reporting', and a completely inaccurate statement.[1]

Williamson, during those long hours, would have been under a considerable emotional strain. It must by that time have occurred to him that if this confession was really to be trusted, so that nothing could yet go wrong at the woman's trial, there was still a chance of rehabilitation—even possibly of restoration to health—for his old friend and admired chief, Jonathan Whicher. He must therefore have been most intensely anxious to be quite sure that Constance Kent had no intention to ruin everything by retracting from her confession. He must have needed that reassurance, and—however strong were the effects of his training in the matter of 'official reticence'—he was alone with the woman, in a locked railway compartment, where nothing that was said could be overheard.

It therefore seems only reasonable to assume that the journey was *not* 'conducted in complete silence'. And if so, we need have no difficulty in guessing at the lines of the conversation, for Constance Kent subsequently published a full confession, in words which would have given the exact answers to Williamson's urgent questions. . . .

'You did murder that child? You really did?'

'Yes. I did.'

'Why did you do it?'

'I felt I was under the influence of the Devil. Of course, he is behind every wicked action, isn't he? Do you know that I hadn't said my prayers for a year?'

[1] Alas, the newspapers of that day were not entirely faultless. *The Times* in its obituary notice of Williamson, describes him as having been 'in charge' of the case of the murder of Lord William Russell—which occurred when Williamson was 9 years old.

Inspector Williamson would not have understood about the Devil. You heard about him in Church—but not in criminal cases.

'But—but did you hate the child? It can't have been true when you told Inspector Whicher that you were fond of the boy and that you played with him on the day he—the day you killed him?'

'Oh yes, that was quite true. I was very fond of little Francis. I didn't want to hurt him.'

'Then it was his mother you wanted to hurt?'

'Oh no, I was fond of my stepmother, too. She was always kind to me. But sometimes disparaging things were said about us—the first family of my father—and I stored them up and knew I had to avenge them. I know now that that was the Devil talking to me. He told me I should have to kill one of the children, because of those things that had been said. It had to be Francis, of course, because everyone was so fond of him. I don't think I *hurt* him, you know. It was quite quick.'

It was impossible not to shudder at such a statement.

'How—how did you do it?'

'With one of my father's razors. I had taken it out of his wardrobe a few days before.'

'A few days before? Then—you mean that this wasn't done on the spur of the moment?'

'Oh no. The Devil had been prompting me for weeks. In the end, I took the razor, and I hid candles and matches in the closet, so as to be able to see what I was doing. Then on the night when I was going to do it, I undressed and went to bed—I had to do that because I expected my sisters to come and say good night, and it would have looked so odd if I had still been dressed—

and then, soon after midnight, when I thought everyone would be asleep, I got up.'

It was uncanny. This was exactly what Jonathan Whicher had argued about her—she seemed to be using his very words.

'At one time, I had thought it would be better to dress; only then I realised that it would look peculiar if Elizabeth—the nursemaid—woke up and saw me in the nursery in my clothes at that time of night. So I did it all in my nightdress. I suppose I ought to have felt cold when I was crossing the garden, but I didn't feel anything at all: probably the Devil saw to that, so that I shouldn't be deterred from what he wanted me to do.'

'Go on, go on!'

'The first thing I did—and this was as soon as my father had retired to his bedroom—was to go downstairs to unbolt the drawing-room door and open the window into the garden. I had to do that first, while my hands were empty. Then I went up to the nursery, and took little Francis from his cot. Just for one moment I thought Elizabeth was going to wake up, but I suppose the Devil was seeing to that, too. She just rolled over in bed, without opening her eyes.

'I carried Francis through the garden to the closet, and there I did it, with the razor. He didn't even wake up, you know, so he can't have felt anything.'

If she had been raving, with straws in her hair, it would not have sounded so terrible. But she spoke quite calmly. In her black clothes, with the veil pushed back, her face had that calm serenity which one sees in the faces of nuns.

'Then I went back to the bedroom. I wanted to go straight off to sleep, because I was very tired, but I thought I ought to make sure first that there weren't any traces. Such a nuisance it was, too: I found two tiny spots of blood on my nightdress.'

So Jonathan Whicher had been right about the nightdress, too! Though he had worked without evidence and only 'on the basis of improbable suspicions', he had been right on every single point.

'I washed the nightdress and hung it out to dry. But in the morning, the two spots still showed, faintly. I knew the police would come, and I thought if they saw bloodstains on my nightdress they would know I had done it. So I decided to burn the nightdress, pretending it had been lost in the wash. I told the maid to put it in the basket with the other soiled linen, and then when she had gone to fetch me a glass of water I took it out again and hid it in my bedroom. Oh, and I wiped the razor and put it back where it had come from. Later, I burnt the nightdress in my grate and put the ashes into the kitchen stove, when no one could see me.'

It was almost word for word what Jonathan Whicher had said. Williamson had spent hours, searching—amongst other things—for ashes and for recognisable fragments of material in them. . . .

He would not have been able to resist saying something to Constance Kent about Whicher.

'Yes. He was very clever. I couldn't believe anyone could be so clever and find out so much, after all the precautions I had taken. At first I had quite a shock when Elizabeth was arrested: I hadn't thought of anything like that happening, I mean I hadn't thought of someone else being accused of what I had done. I felt very terrible about it, even though I couldn't see how they could possibly produce any evidence, seeing that she was absolutely innocent. Only I didn't know anything about what happened when people were arrested by the police, and I decided that if she were convicted I would have to confess, so as to save her. But when they said she hadn't done it, and they set her free, I thought everything was sure to be all right. So you can imagine how terrible it was for me when Inspector Whicher came and arrested me.'

'Yet now you are confessing——?'

'Oh yes. I am telling everything. You see, I have learnt that it is my duty to fight the Devil and all his ways.'

5

On the following day, Sergeant Thomas of the Detective Department travelled from London to help Inspector Williamson in the preparation of his case against Constance Kent—just as, five years before, Williamson himself had come to help Inspector Whicher.

When the case reached the Assizes, if the prisoner insisted, after warning, in pleading 'Guilty', no evidence would be produced and conviction would follow automatically; but in the Magistrates' Court, before that, the charge had to be fully supported with all the necessary witnesses. One of these, unavoidably, was Inspector Whicher.

Many a man, in those circumstances, would have been triumphant. Here was his chance to have his character and reputation completely vindicated. Representatives of the newspapers which had previously decried him would be in Court, he could stand out in public, and subsequently in the columns of the newspapers, as a much-wronged man who had been proved by the turn of

Fortune's wheel to be right in every detail. Then, of course, he would have to be reinstated in his old position—or, at the least, if his health did not allow of that, there would be apologies from Sir Richard Mayne and everything possible would be done to make amends to him.

To bring all that about, he had only to say, when in the witness box, 'You see, I was right.' Just a word or two about himself, and the newspaper reporters would see their chance to arouse popular sentiment on his behalf.

Jonathan Whicher, however, was too big a man for that. His evidence was given formally. . . .

'On Sunday, July 15th, 1860 . . . I received directions from Sir Richard Mayne . . . On July 16th, I sent for Miss Constance . . . On the 20th, the warrant, which I now produce, was issued for her apprehension . . . I made every search of the grounds and premises with a view to finding the missing nightdress, but was unsuccessful.'

He said nothing in extenuation of himself, nothing to press home the fact that he was now justified in a sense of triumph. If he had any such sense of triumph, he certainly showed not the slightest sign of it. He looked infirm,[1] but he bore himself with quiet dignity.

From *The Times* of April 27th, 1865:

'Miss Kent was dressed in deep mourning and wore a thick veil, but she looked very much flushed on entering the justice room, and this was increased upon her taking her place at the bar, where every person in a most densely crowded court had an opportunity of gazing at her. . . . During the reading of the confession the prisoner burst into tears—the first time she had exhibited any emotion.'

[1] He died a few years later.

Inevitably, now that the evidence was supported by that confession, the case went to the Assizes. There, the proceedings were very brief.

From *The Times* of July 22nd, 1865:

'Mr. Justice Willes, having put on the black cap, then said with manifest emotion, "I can entertain no doubt, after having read the evidence, and considering it in connection with your three confessions of crime, that your plea is the plea of a guilty person. You appear to have allowed feelings of jealousy and anger to have worked in your breast, until at last they assumed over you the influence and power of the Evil One."

'(Here the learned judge was deeply affected, and spoke in accents broken with emotion. The prisoner was likewise completely overcome by her feelings and, almost turning round in the dock, sobbed audibly.)

'. . . The learned judge then, in the usual terms, passed the awful sentence of the law upon the prisoner, who, after standing for a short time in the dock, covered her face with her veil and was conducted out of court.'[1]

6

The newspapers of the time published leading articles on the case, in which sympathy was offered to Constance Kent's father and to the nurse, against both of whom suspicion had continually been raised during the five

[1] As the murder had been committed when Constance Kent was only sixteen, she was in due course reprieved, her sentence being commuted to one of penal servitude for life. She passed twenty years in prison. A prison governor who had her in his custody (Major Arthur Griffiths) describes her then as 'A small, mouse-like little creature . . . this insignificant, inoffensive little person'. There is no certainty as to what happened to her after her discharge in 1885.

years since the crime had been committed: and a year after the conviction, a public subscription was started for the father's benefit.

But nothing was said about Inspector Whicher, nor about the conduct of the Detective Department at Great Scotland Yard. That was all forgotten. The Metropolitan Police had survived the first notable crisis in its history, and had indeed emerged from it with new strength. A new system of work, giving far greater efficiency and far less chance of disaster, had been evolved as a result of Jonathan Whicher's over-zeal and haste. The growth and skill of the Detective Department would doubtless have continued to increase without check, if a fresh and far greater crisis had not developed within the next twelve years.

PART THREE

The Second Crisis

CHAPTER 8

The Intervening Years

1

Eight years had passed since Inspector Williamson escorted Constance Kent to Trowbridge—nine had passed since Inspector Tanner and Sergeant Clarke brought Franz Muller from America. In those years there had been what the newspapers of the time would have called 'sweeping changes' at Great Scotland Yard.

Sir Richard Mayne was dead. Foolishly—but characteristically—he had refused to let even old age drive him from his job, and consequently he had remained Commissioner of Police until he was well into his seventies and quite unable to do his work efficiently: on one occasion of a public riot, when he should have seemed fully in command of the situation, he was referred to by a contemporary writer as 'the poor old fellow'. It would have been better for his memory if he had gone while the going was good.

Mayne had been succeeded by Colonel Edmund Henderson, a new broom who not only swept clean but also swept expansively. One of the most striking things he did, right at the start of his eighteen years as Commissioner, was to bring in the system of divisional detectives. No longer was all crime detection in London to be done from Whitehall: each of the other sixteen divisions now had its own independent Detective Department of about ten men. At the same time, the Department at Great Scotland Yard was increased in strength from fifteen men to forty-two.

In general, the new system meant that minor crimes could be dealt with by the men on the spot, but when any important case occurred, one or more officers from Great Scotland Yard would work with the divisional detectives, it being always understood that the Department supplied the real experts. At that period, the divisional detectives were not 'under' the head of the Department, but all were answerable to the Commissioner of Police.

There were drastic changes, too, in the Detective Department.

Inspector Tanner had become ill, had retired to run an inn in Winchester, and then had soon died. On his retirement, he had been replaced by the two best of the sergeants, James J. Thomson and George Clarke. But within a year of that promotion, Inspector Thomson distinguished himself over a notable arrest and was rewarded by being made Superintendent in charge of E Division of the ordinary police.

The number of inspectors then rose to six—Clarke, Palmer, Druscovich, Shore, Pay and Mulvaney—and Frederick Williamson became Superintendent and the head of the Department. In the next six or seven years, there were changes in the Inspectors' List (Pay died and Mulvaney dropped out, and Sayer came in, to remain), but from 1869 until 1876 the vital 'backbone' of the

Detective Department consisted of Superintendent Williamson and his chief and completely trusted assistants, Clarke, Palmer, Druscovich and Shore. It is four of these five men who are the principal actors in the second act of this drama.

2

During the years immediately before the rising of the curtain, the Department had had to deal with certain activities which were not quite those for which it had been created. They were not, in the narrower sense of the word, 'criminal', although in a wider sense—and in their effect—they were very criminal indeed, for they involved murder—and also 'destructive outrages' which caused a large number of casualties.

A secret society, known as the Fenians, had been set up in America to support the cause of Home Rule for Ireland. When the American Civil War ended in 1865, a large number of arms, and large quantities of explosives, were set free, and some of these came into Fenian hands. There were thus armed fanatics to serve (if it did serve) the Irish cause. They came, mostly, from America by way of Ireland to London, Liverpool and Manchester.

They have been described as not being criminal in the narrower sense of that word because they were not actuated by motives of personal gain and they were all political 'idealists': at any rate, whatever may be said about that—and whatever *was* said in the English newspapers of the time—they had hardly the ordinary criminal mentality. Consequently, the Detective Department found itself faced with new problems. For one thing, no true Fenian could ever be persuaded by the police to betray other Fenians; and for another thing, whenever a Fenian was arrested, there was always an attempt at rescue.

In this political 'war', the important thing, obviously, was to arrest the Fenian leaders. (It was for one such arrest that Inspector Thomson won his promotion to Superintendent.) Two arrested Fenians were being conveyed across Manchester in a prison van, when the guards were attacked by five men, and in the ensuing scuffle a police-sergeant was shot dead. Within a few months of that crime, a cask of gunpowder was exploded against the wall of the Clerkenwell 'House of Correction' in which certain Irish leaders were confined: and although an escape was averted, four people in neighbouring houses were killed and forty others, including a number of children who had been playing in the street, were 'shockingly mutilated'.

Naturally, at such a time, it became the practice for any crime for which a delinquent could not be found to be attributed to the Fenians: as well as being the natural thing, it was often, perhaps, the easiest way of excusing a failure.

Consequently, the records of that time show a large number of 'Fenian outrages'—some of which have all the look of commonplace assaults—and comparatively few ordinary crimes. Consequently, too, Williamson and his men were continually journeying to Liverpool and Manchester when they might have been sufficiently employed among the regular criminals of London. They had an exhausting task, for which they were not particularly well fitted.[1]

[1] It was not until several years later that 'The Irish Branch' was created, especially to deal with Fenian activities, in charge of Inspector Littlechild. Later, the Irish Branch widened its responsibilities and became known, as at present, as 'The Special Branch'.

3

By 1872, however, there was a temporary lull in Fenian activities and the Detective Department was more able to concentrate on its ordinary work.

In that year a case was dealt with which shows the limitations under which the detectives of that time had to work.

A Mrs. Squires and her daughter—the mother being a widow aged 76 and the daughter a woman of 48—lived alone in a house in Hoxton, where they carried on business as stationers and newsagents. On a certain Wednesday afternoon in July, a small boy came to the shop to buy a paper, and found it empty. He thought it a good opportunity to look at all the exciting things which were laid out on the counter: but when he stood on tiptoe to do so, he found that the top of the counter was soaked in blood.

Terrified, he ran from the shop and brought in a neighbour. Then, the dead body of old Mrs. Squires was found lying in a pool of blood behind the counter: and in the doorway leading to the basement stairs was found that of the daughter. Both of them had been beaten to death with blows on the head.

The police were called and Inspector Ramsey of N Division took charge of the case. He was joined by Inspector William Palmer and Sergeant Lansdowne of the Detective Department and the pursuit of the murderer began . . . or rather, the enquiry began, with confident expectation that 'pursuit' would soon follow.

It was found that the whole house had been ransacked, which established robbery as the motive for the crime. There was, of course, no evidence as to what had been stolen, but it appeared that, unless the thief had gone in for wanton damage, he must have been looking for some particular article: cushions had been ripped up, and even the clock had been torn from the nail on which it hung on the wall.

4

The first difficulty in what might have promised to prove an easy case arose from the fact that there were a number of very odd contradictions in the evidence.

Inspector Palmer would doubtless have gone to report them to Superintendent Williamson. . . .

'Most extremely odd, it is, sir. I can't make head nor tail of it all. For one thing, there's that clock that was pulled off the wall and dropped: it has stopped at 12 o'clock, which ought to mean that that's when it was torn down—in which case the women in the shop must have been dead by then, killed before that. But I've got a reliable witness who swears he saw the old lady standing at her shop door at 12.30.

'Then there's another odd thing. By the look of it all, someone was looking for something special: a hoard of money, perhaps, if he was an ordinary thief, or the old lady's will if he was someone special like a relation. But whichever he was, he didn't get either of those things, for all his thorough search, because the money *and* the will were both stuffed down the side of the sofa, and left there. So what I want to know is why he stopped looking—why, after all that trouble, he didn't go on till he found what he wanted. It doesn't seem to make sense, doing all that, including a couple of murders, and then going off without much to show for it. I mean, it isn't as if he panicked, because he didn't: he stayed to do all that searching.

'And there's more still than that. If there's anything in that idea of mine that someone was after the will, then the most obvious person is a son who is in Colney Hatch. Only it isn't likely, they say there, that he'd have had the chance to get over the wall and nip out and get back again. And anyway, apart from that, we've found hairs in the younger woman's fingers, as if she'd fought someone and pulled his hair out—and the hair's grey, so it came off someone who is old or oldish, whereas this son at Colney Hatch is quite a young man. Really, sir, I don't know what to make of it."

It was one of Frederick Williamson's special attributes that he had a power of grasping essentials and ignoring redundancies. 'No matter the intricacy of a case,' says Chief-Inspector Littlechild, 'he immediately gripped its points and required but ten words of explanation when others asked for fifty.' So he would very quickly have cut his way through Inspector Palmer's statement of difficulties.

'You needn't bother about the clock, Inspector,' he would have said. 'It may have been "wrong" or they may have forgotten to wind it, so that it stopped before it was torn down. The clock may therefore be regarded as irrelevant. The son in Colney Hatch seems to me to be irrelevant also—you can forget about him. I'll give you a better point than either of those. If there was blood all over the counter and the floor, there must have been a good deal on the murderer as well. I understand that nothing was found to suggest that he washed his face and hands before he left: therefore he must have been extremely noticeable. He cannot have gone far through the streets, at mid-day, in that state, without being noticed. He wasn't noticed: therefore he didn't go far. In that case, he is probably a near neighbour of Mrs. Squires.'

'There's plenty of people round Hoxton way who would have done a thing like that. Inspector Ramsay tells me——'

'Of course. There are plenty of people everywhere who'd do a thing like that. If there weren't, you wouldn't be here.'

'I meant a bit more than that, sir. Inspector Ramsay tells me that someone tried to break into Mrs. Squires' house on Saturday night—early on Sunday morning, that is, three days before the murder.'

'Tell me about that. And keep it brief, Inspector.'

'The old dame woke up and heard someone. She put on a light and yelled from the window. The thief or thieves then ran, and nothing was taken.'

'I see,' Williamson would have said. 'And that particularly interests you? In other words, your theory is that the thief who failed to get in on Sunday succeeded on Wednesday. If that is so—and perhaps anyway—it does begin to look as if the motive wasn't ordinary robbery. There cannot have been much worth stealing in that house, and if somebody thought it worth while to come twice . . . I think we are making some progress, Inspector. You now have to look for an elderly man living in the immediate neighbourhood who wanted a particular article from that house.'

It has been said of Frederick Williamson that he treated his subordinates with tact and encouraged them to persevere in cases which seemed incapable of solution. That that encouragement not only removed Inspector Palmer's worried lack of self-confidence, but also made him convinced of success, is shown by the announcement, inspired by the Inspector, which appeared in the Press on the following day:

'There is further important evidence in the hands of the police pointing strongly to a suspected person, whose arrest was last night thought to be only a question of a few hours.'

5

Nevertheless the search by Inspector Palmer and his team of detectives for 'an elderly man living in the immediate neighbourhood' proved entirely unproductive. It seemed that all the grey-haired men in that part of Hoxton had either alibis, or good characters, or else an entire absence of motive.

By the next day, the limits of the search were considerably narrowed when the doctor reported in detail on his examination of the wounds. There were nine of these on the head of the old lady and fifteen on the daughter, all on the temple. They had been made by some kind of blunt, wooden instrument. And in the wounds were found traces of builders' plaster.

The inference from that, of course, was that the weapon had been a plasterer's hammer; and that was borne out to some extent by the discovery of a bloodstained apron. But the number of grey-haired plasterers living in that immediate neighbourhood was very small indeed: and there certainly wasn't one of them who was open to suspicion of having committed that crime.

So the search dragged on for some days. Then, very belatedly, there appeared a fresh witness.

At about one o'clock on the Wednesday afternoon, the day of the crime, it had happened that two wagons, each with a team of three horses, had come from opposite directions down the road and had been on the point of passing each other just outside Mrs. Squires' shop. The driver of one of them, a man named Randall, now came to report that just at that moment the door of the shop had opened, and a man had run out and tried to dash across the road between the two approaching horses. There had been very little room, and in his haste the man had stumbled against the boy who was leading the fore horse of Randall's team. Both the boy and the man had gone to the ground. . . .

Inspector Palmer, when he had heard that much of the story, would have been excited. 'You noticed what this man was like?'

'Well, sir, there weren't much time and I was angry, seeing my lad knocked over. I was for getting down from my box to handle the chap.'

'Yes, yes. But you saw him. You must be able to describe him.'

'Oh ay, I saw him, I did. He went down a wallop on the road, and sarve him right, for knocking my lad down. And when he got up, he'd got his trousers torn right across at the left knee.'

That, of course, was not the kind of detail that Inspector Palmer wanted, a grey-haired plasterer with torn trousers being no easier to find than a grey-haired plasterer with whole trousers, when there were no grey-haired plasterers to be suspected!

'His face, man, his face!'

'Oh, I didn't see his face, sir. Pulled his hat down over his eyes, he did, as soon as he got up, and kept his face away. Very careful of something in his pocket he was being, too: kept his left hand in it all the time, even when he went over. No, I didn't see his face, not to notice. But a youngish man, he was, and black-haired.'

6

The case was insoluble. When at last he was convinced that he would never be able to find the black-haired plasterer who had had grey hairs pulled from his head by his victim, Inspector Palmer would have gone again to Superintendent Williamson. . . .

'There's nothing to go on, sir, not a real clue anywhere.'

'Clues don't have to be real, Inspector, if they are tangible. You've been over the house again and found nothing fresh?'

'Only a stud. That was found on the floor when the bloodstains were being washed off. It was behind the counter, so it can't have come from a customer: must have been the murderer's, seeing that women don't wear such things. But where's that going to take us?'

'You're sure there's nothing more useful? Nothing to help us to identify the man?'

Inspector Palmer would have laughed at that. 'All we've got is a picture of his thumb. Two pictures of it, really. He left them on a couple of maps, where the blood was spilt. Beautiful pictures of thumbs, they are, with all the fancy lines on the skin. But what's the use of that? We can't identify a man from his thumb-print, can we?'

Probably Superintendent Williamson would have laughed, too, at the absurdity of that notion.

So the man who killed Mrs. Squires and her daughter was never found. The problem was too difficult a one for the Detective Department. It is described by Lansdowne, who worked on it as Inspector Palmer's sergeant, as a mysterious murder to which there was not a single clue: 'there was positively nothing to go upon'. But if it had occurred about twenty-five years later, and the murderer had left the same perfect impressions of his thumb-prints——!

7

Frederick Williamson was at that time 41. He had already achieved the ambition of his boyhood, to be a Superintendent and the head of the Detective Department. But it is very doubtful if he had much time to realise the fact.

Colonel Henderson appreciated Williamson's qualities and experience, and therefore did not keep as close a rein on the Detective Department as Sir Richard Mayne had done in his last years. Thus Inspector Lansdowne says, 'Mr. Williamson for a good many years had a comparatively free hand in his department', and Sir Robert Anderson says that during the ten years from 1868 to 1878 the success of the Department was mainly due to him. He had, in fact, entirely adopted Mayne's new system of work, with himself in control of it: he appointed one of his inspectors to handle each case—but always under his own supervision—and then allowed the inspectors to delegate parts of the work to their sergeants. Frequent reports had to be written by the inspectors and they all came before Superintendent Williamson, who annotated them with his own suggestions and ideas and then returned them. 'He had,' says Lansdowne, 'a special gift for wading through a mass of documents to discover the points, and his notes and directions were always practical and sensible.'

For all his quick success, Williamson was a modest man with a sense of humour. Up to that time, he had always managed to keep alive his private interests—the river, the rose-garden and his family—however great was the pressure of his work. It has been said that, at any rate up to 1877, he never missed watching the Oxford and Cambridge Boat Race. In 1872 he had just acquired the house (No. 4 Smith Square, Westminster) in which he lived with his growing family for the rest of his life, and it was in its small garden that he grew the roses for which he was famous in that neighbourhood.

These years were probably the happiest of his life. He had success and he had friends: the two together would have given him a sense of contentment.

'Few but the initiated recognised the redoubtable detective in the quiet, unpretending, middle-aged man who walked leisurely along Whitehall, balancing a hat that was a little too large for him loosely on his head, and often with a sprig of a leaf or a flower between his lips.'[1]

8

Clarke, Palmer and Druscovich were made Chief-Inspectors in 1870, and for nearly seven years they were Superintendent Williamson's right-hand men, taking a lot of the work off his shoulders. Everything went well —or seemed to be going well—then.

Frederick Williamson must often have felt that in the course of that grim business called life he had been particularly lucky to have such good fellows to work with: first, the boys with whom, as a sergeant, he had gone on 'barneys', then Jonathan Whicher, then Richard Tanner, then James J. Thomson—and now George Clarke, William Palmer and Nat Druscovich.

Of those last three, the one who was much the closest to him was George Clarke. Clarke was a dozen years older

[1] Arthur Griffiths.

than Williamson, but that would not have mattered. They were near neighbours, in Westminster, and the two men, with their wives, were on 'visiting terms at home'. Later, Williamson was able to say, 'I have known Chief-Inspector Clarke for over twenty years: he was my most confidential and trusted assistant.' But that, of course, was only of the official association between them. There was also a bond of personal friendship which was of much greater importance.

CHIEF-INSPECTOR GEORGE CLARKE

"A 'good sort', dependable (up to a point) and highly intelligent"

CHAPTER 9

Easy Money for All

1

In 1873, there was a very heavy crop of swindles connected with the Turf: the people who backed horses wanted easy money, and were therefore likely to be gullible—and not to ask too many questions—when they were told of a 'system' by which they could get it.

Chief-Inspector Clarke had become something of a specialist in dealing with that form of crime: he had achieved the proud record of having got no less than seventy-one racing swindlers convicted and sentenced to imprisonment. Unfortunately, however, there were always plenty of fresh swindlers to take the place of those who had been put away. Moreover, criminals, like the rest of the world, had a way of learning by other people's mistakes. Thus Clarke found it continually growing more and more difficult to catch the people he was after.

The methods used by these swindlers were often extremely ingenious: particularly, they had the 'technique of approach' worked out to a nicety.

'What I can never see,' Chief-Inspector Clarke might have said about it, 'is why everyone in the country isn't a millionaire. It's so easy making money—on horses. And you can't lose. At least, that's what it says in these circulars I have to spend my time reading.

'Of course, betting with the bookies is quite out-of-date. Nowadays, it is done through an obliging gentleman with a system, who guarantees that you can't lose. Or else with a Philanthropic Society which only exists to protect you from throwing away your money. "The Systematic Investment Society" or "The General Society for Insurance against Losses on the Turf": that sort of thing. Wonderful, the titles these gentlemen think up! And then there's the nice way they invite you to give them your money. Listen to this: "The Directors of the Society are desirous of placing before the public the only means by which they can amass a large fortune in a short time without risk." That's cunning, that is. If "they" means the public, as anyone would think, it's a downright lie and swindle: but take it the other way, with "they" meaning the Directors of the Society, and every word of it is true. There's no risk at all to the Directors of the Society—unless I can catch up with them. And that is becoming uncommonly difficult.'

2

Advertisements containing such appealing phrases were printed in the newspapers, and circulars were posted to 'likely clients'. Thousands of people were taken in and sent their money, either delivering it personally at the 'office' or sending it by post. For that they got a receipt —but nothing more. After a few weeks, the clients began to complain. But if they called at the offices, they found everything locked up and empty: if they wrote, their letters came back marked 'Gone away, no address'. The birds had flown, with a haul of money which had never been placed on any horse at all.

Then, within a week or two, a fresh flood of circulars and advertisements would be poured out, with the name of another Society and another address, in a different city—but with the same style of invitation to amass a quick fortune without risk. Those people who had been caught before would probably—but not inevitably—be shy of the appeal: but there were always plenty of 'mugs' who would say, 'Oh yes, I've heard that there are swindlers doing this kind of business, but this advertisement looks absolutely genuine. . . .'

3

The main difficulty experienced by Chief-Inspector Clarke was one of speed. He had three weeks at the most in which to learn that a swindle had started, to prove that it was a swindle, to get the necessary evidence, and to pounce. If the police came too late, they had to start all over again, because though they might be convinced that the G.H.I. Society in Glasgow was run by the men who, a short time before, had run the D.E.F. Association in Manchester, and before that the A.B.C. Turf Philanthropic Society in London, it was very difficult to prove it. In fact, fresh evidence had to be collected each time.

Not only that, but the gangs of swindlers sometimes cut their losses and disappeared after one week, or even after a day or two. That was when they became wise to the fact that the police were on their trail.

4

This class of detective work was peculiarly difficult because it was no use making a raid on offices when there was no certainty of securing enough evidence for an arrest: the only effect of such a raid would be to warn the criminals to disappear. The task, therefore, was to obtain information—without giving away the fact that it was being sought.

That could only be done by 'underground' work—by what might be called 'personal contacts' with criminals: Clarke and the men working under him had constantly to mix with them in public houses and other places and discuss with them any subject on earth except racing swindles, while hoping that a word would be let fall which would serve afterwards as a pointer. The criminals, of course, knew perfectly well that the detectives were after information—but they didn't know precisely what information was wanted. There was therefore just a chance that something would be let out.

Something which came out at one such meeting had led to the conviction of a man named Trevelli, who ran a betting office in Croydon. Trevelli had received a sentence of five years penal servitude, so he was now safely out of the way. Some of his confederates, however, were still at large. There was one of them in particular, Henry Walters, whom Clarke very badly wanted to catch.

Though a confirmed criminal, Walters had somehow or other managed to obtain a licence to run a public house called 'The Grapes' in Red Lion Street, Holborn. Red Lion Street, at that time, was on the fringe of the most notorious district in London, and the clientele of 'The

Grapes' was far from select—in fact, it consisted mostly of criminals as double-dyed as the landlord.

Walters could have been extremely useful to the police as a source of information, if he had been willing to talk. But he never was—though Chief-Inspector Clarke always had hopes of him. There was a burglary case in Essex, and Clarke was convinced that Walters knew who had done it. He had the idea that although it would be useless to question Walters at 'The Grapes' on such a matter, something might be learnt if Walters would consent to meet him secretly. If he sent the man a letter, suggesting such a private meeting . . .

But apart from that, Clarke wanted Walters on his own account. He had a very shrewd notion that it was Walters who was running 'The General Society for Insurance against Losses on the Turf'.

5

Advertisements appeared in the papers from a new betting firm—or at any rate a firm under a new name, Philip Gardner and Co., with an address in Scotland. Clarke was convinced that it was being run by a well-known criminal, William Kurr, and this time he was able to act quickly. . . . But not quickly enough. By the time the police arrived, the birds had flown.

Clarke would have reported that failure to Williamson.

'I was sure we had moved fast enough to catch 'em that time, but I was wrong. It beats me how they always know we're coming. I suppose they keep a ring of look-outs and spies, but I don't move the way look-outs and spies would see me. I just don't know how they do it. And I'll tell you another thing, Mr. Williamson. There's another lot I'm after, calling themselves Archer and Co. Sometimes they're in London and sometimes they aren't. All their customers are in France—all we've heard of, that is. And that's particularly difficult for us, because as nobody is going to deliver money by hand, they don't even have to have offices. The clients in France send their money by post to what we find is only an accommodation address. And that's always changing, so we can't fix on anyone.

'Still, in spite of that, I thought we were going to get the better of them when Mr. Druscovich tumbled onto a fellow who was taking a parcel of the circulars to France in order to post 'em there. The arrest was done very quietly, and we ought to have been able to follow it up. But when we did, the gang had gone. They must have heard about the first arrest after all, I suppose, though I can't think how they did.'

'You mean—an ordinary "look-out" couldn't have got the information, couldn't have given you away?'

'Quite impossible in that case, I should say. It worries me a lot, Mr. Williamson. These men are being "tipped off" every time. I'm rather inclined to fancy that there must be one man who is behind more than half of these frauds—a sort of central organisation, you know—and that it is he who is getting the information and sending it where it's wanted. But if so, I don't know who he is. It would have to be someone cleverer than Henry Walters, and cleverer than William Kurr. Cleverer, I should say, than anyone I've met in this type of business yet. And even then, I don't know what the method is. I don't see what the method *can* be: I don't see what method there can be that gives these men information that isn't known to anyone except the police. It is worrying me quite a lot, Mr. Williamson.'

6

It worried Superintendent Williamson also. He made very secret and discreet enquiries himself, and reached the conclusion that Chief-Inspector Clarke's suspicions were well-founded: there wasn't any doubt at all that the criminals in these turf cases had received information which was supposed to be known only to the police-officers concerned.

They had just taken on twenty-seven new recruits: there must be some youngster among them who did not yet realise that he had, above all else, to keep his mouth shut.

Further cautious enquiries showed, however, that the Chief-Inspector had taken every precaution: the recruits were never told anything.

That was a most disturbing discovery. It seemed to mean that someone who ought to know better was being indiscreet.

That danger was inherent in police work. One of the early authorities, when asked by a recruit how he should learn his work as a policeman, had answered 'Get to know thieves, my boy'; and that principle had always been followed. When the detectives were not openly after a particular criminal, there was a sort of truce in which the opposing forces met and exchanged drinks and talked—and listened to each other. Much was learnt, in that way, about the habits and practices of thieves. It was quite normal for a detective to mix on outwardly friendly terms with a gang of criminals—and then to come with a warrant for them a week later. But of course it was essential, in those 'friendly' meetings, that a detective should use his ears and carefully guard his tongue.

The present circumstances forced Williamson to the

conclusion that one of his men was talking far more than he ought to have done. Very far more. For to say, in the presence of criminals, 'We have arrested Henry Street, while he was on his way to France with a parcel of racing circulars', when it had been laid down that that fact was highly secret, was considerably more than an indiscretion. It wasn't the kind of thing that would 'slip out': it was a definite statement, a clear infringement of orders.

7

The Superintendent's secret enquiries continued. If that kind of thing were really happening, he had to discover who was doing it.

He did not have to bother, of course, about the Chief-Inspectors: it was unthinkable that either Clarke, Druscovich or Palmer could have done such a thing as this. Nor was it possible in the case of old John Shore, the most experienced of the three inspectors. It was a relief to find that the other two inspectors—Sayer and Davey, who had only recently been promoted—had not been engaged on the cases in which there had been a leakage of information. Therefore the source of the trouble must rest among the sergeants and constables. That was at any rate a little better than it being an inspector.

There was, as it happened, one fact which helped in this secret enquiry. While most of the turf cases that had gone wrong had been under Clarke, one—that in which Henry Street, the messenger to France, was arrested—had been under Druscovich. For the most part, Clarke and Druscovich used a different set of assistants, but if Druscovich had on that particular occasion used one of Clarke's men——

Frederick Williamson discovered that that had actually happened. There was one man, and one only, who had been in every one of the suspected cases: Sergeant John Meiklejohn.[1]

But Meiklejohn was a senior sergeant, high on the list for promotion to inspector, and a thoroughly experienced man. It just wasn't conceivable—well, it was hardly conceivable—that he could have been careless in a way that would have been shameful in a raw recruit.

Yet what other conclusion could now be reached?

8

If it had not been for his memory of Jonathan Whicher, who had brought ignominy upon himself by making an arrest first and looking for the evidence afterwards—and if he had not been a scrupulously fair-minded man—Williamson might have asked the Commissioner to dismiss Sergeant Meiklejohn from the Force, or at least to suspend him. But he was not the man to do that when there was absolutely no tangible evidence, apart from what might conceivably be only coincidence. Instead, therefore, he allowed matters to run on, and only decided that for the present he would have to depart from his usual practice of leaving betting cases in the hands of Chief-Inspector Clarke, and keep them closely under his own eye.

Most of Clarke's attention at that time was occupied by the 'General Society for Insurance Against Losses on the

[1] Meiklejohn's antecedents are unknown; but in 1869, as a detective-sergeant, he assisted Inspector James J. Thomson in a case of double murder at Poplar. That case ended in the murderer's suicide before capture. Meiklejohn does not appear to have done anything outstandingly successful in his career: but on the other hand there was nothing in any way against him.

Turf'. That swindle was being conducted on a very big scale. Advertisements appeared in newspapers in Germany, France, Italy, Switzerland and Russia, announcing a bona-fide betting system which could not fail and which was therefore being conducted for the public benefit by this Philanthropic Society with its imposing list of Directors. Clarke had looked very carefully at that list of Directors. Not a single name on it was genuine, that is to say, some of the people (including the President, a 'Lord Lennox') did not exist at all, while the others, although existing, had never heard of the Society or lent their names to any such concern. And although the advertisements announced, impressively, 'Bankers: the Bank of England', the Society had no account there, nor—at any rate in its own name—with any other bank.

The method of operation was much the same as in the other cases, but on a bigger scale and more specious.

The advertisements said that the way to make money on the turf was to avoid the well-known meetings and bet on the smaller ones. As a principle, of course, that was nonsense; but Clarke realised that there was a very sound reason behind it. All the money sent to the Society came from abroad, from the countries in which the advertisements appeared, that having the advantage, to its promoters, of ensuring a delay before enquiries could be made by dissatisfied clients. The longer the delay, the more time there was to collect a good haul before the offices were closed. But to ensure that delay it was essential to avoid letting the foreign clients think that their money was being put on horses running in big races, such as the Derby, the winners of which were announced in newspapers abroad. The friendly advice to 'avoid the well-known meetings and bet on the smaller ones' resulted in

INSPECTOR JOHN MEIKLEJOHN

"It wasn't conceivable that he could have been careless"

only one thing: that the clients remained completely in the dark as to what had happened to their money.

Ingenuity was shown, too, in getting in as much money as possible. For instance, in January a client in Russia sent to the Society 100 roubles. The Society thereupon sent back a very specious letter—which was intercepted by the English police—saying that that bet had 'unfortunately' been delayed in the post and had not arrived until February 2nd; and that in February the Society was not accepting any bets for less than 200 roubles, because it was going to be a particularly good month. So would the client kindly send 100 roubles more, to put the matter in order!

This Society was being run—for the distinguished Directors—by someone who signed letters as 'Sidney Montague'. There was also a Secretary named 'Will Osborne'. Chief-Inspector Clarke felt fairly certain that both names were aliases for Henry Walters—although one of them might be being used, part of the time, or all the time, by another criminal named Edwin Murray. But being 'fairly certain' was of no use to Clarke. If he obtained a warrant for the arrest of Walters and Murray, they would plead complete ignorance of the whole matter, asking what evidence there was that they were in any way connected with people named Montague and Osborne. And there was no evidence of that at all: it was merely 'extremely probable'.

9

As there was no evidence, and no means of looking for any, the only thing to be done was to wait hopefully for something useful to happen. That method usually failed, of course: but in this instance the evidence did arrive.

Its coming was pure chance: it was brought by someone who had no idea that he was bringing it.

A Mr. Daniel Portch came to Great Scotland Yard in order to charge four men with assault. One of the men was Henry Walters, another was William Kurr. The names of the other two were not known.

As soon as Walters was mentioned, the matter was put before Superintendent Williamson, who called in Chief-Inspector Clarke and then took over the interview. Very soon, he extracted from Mr. Portch the full story.

He was a friend, he said, of a Captain Berkeley, 'a racing man' who knew Henry Walters and had 'done some business' with him. In connection with this business, Captain Berkeley had received two letters from Walters —or, to be more exact, two identical copies of the same letter, but bearing different signatures.

Williamson would have pricked up his ears at that. 'What were the two signatures?'

One copy of the letter, Mr. Portch explained, was signed by Henry Walters himself. The other bore the signature of somebody named Osborne—'Will Osborne'.

Mr. Portch's explanation of that curious happening was that it was just a careless mistake in the office. A draft of the reply would have been written out, and each of the two men would have made a fair copy of it, adding his own signature, without knowing what the other man was doing.

That, of course, was possible—provided that there were two men and not only one. On the other hand, it was equally possible that Walters had made the first copy with his own signature and posted it, and then—forgetting what he had already done—had written it out again over the false 'Osborne' signature.

But it didn't really matter—to Superintendent Williamson and Chief-Inspector Clarke. The only thing that mattered to them was this tremendous piece of luck which was bringing into their hands two identical letters with the different signatures, to prove beyond all doubt the association of Henry Walters with 'Will Osborne'.

But that was not by any means the end of the story.

Walters had very quickly realised the mistake he had made—and that if those two letters ever fell into the hands of the police, the 'Society for Insurance against Losses on the Turf' would go out of business, while he himself would pass from the sight of his fellow-men for six years or so. He had therefore approached Captain Berkeley and asked him to be good enough to return the two letters, 'now that he had finished reading them'.

Unfortunately for him, Captain Berkeley, though not actually known to the police, was distinctly 'fly': as astute as a man had to be to make a living on the turf and not let his winnings be stolen from him. He had no idea why Walters wanted the letters back—though perhaps he could have guessed at that, if he had thought very hard—but the fact that they were asked for meant that they were of value—to Walters. He therefore said 'business is business' and suggested that he should be paid £500 for returning them.

That, it appeared, was where Henry Walters made his great mistake. Six years of freedom from prison would have been cheap to him at £500—a mere drop in the ocean of money he was getting from the Society—but he was probably annoyed at the way Captain Berkeley was 'holding him up' and he decided to pay back in the same coin. He therefore agreed to pay the £500 and instructed the Captain to bring the letters to the Cock Tavern in Highbury, where the money would be given him. And at the same time he suggested privately to three of his friends—hefty fellows—that they might join him in a little spree at the Cock Tavern.

Captain Berkeley knew Walters fairly well, but not well enough. He thought it wise to take with him an escort on the expedition—but it didn't occur to him that half a dozen of his friends wouldn't be too many. So he only took this Mr. Daniel Portch.

Portch, apparently, wasn't much good in a fight, anyway. He managed to preserve his own skin—probably because no one was particularly interested in him—but he didn't protect his friend. Captain Berkeley was badly 'beaten up' and the letters were taken from him.

10

From Mr. Portch's description, Clarke was able to identify one of the unnamed men as Edwin Murray. Warrants were therefore obtained against Murray, Henry Walters and William Kurr, on a charge of assault, the idea being that once the men were under lock and key, more evidence could be collected to connect some at least of them with the 'Society for Insurance'. The incriminating letters, of course, would not be found: but both Mr. Portch and Captain Berkeley (when he had recovered from his wounds) would be able to give evidence of having seen them. Meanwhile, the important thing was to get the arrests made without any hitch.

Every possible precaution was taken. Walters and Murray were arrested. But when the detectives reached the house of William Kurr, they found that he had fled.

Once again, a leading criminal had received news and disappeared.

Despite everything, something had slipped up. There was no proof that Sergeant Meiklejohn had known of the arrests before they happened, but on the other hand neither was there certainty that he could not have known. Too many people had known, and there might have been harmless gossip within the walls of Scotland Yard. . . . But that, of course, would have been a very different matter from the passing of the news to criminals. Really, that would have been more than merely not guarding one's tongue, more than mere indiscretion——

But still there was no definite evidence, against Meiklejohn or anyone else.

Probably Superintendent Williamson was still too honest, too fair-minded, too much impressed by his memories, and too anxious not to commit an act of gross injustice. He ought, certainly, at that point to have taken action, of one sort or another, against Meiklejohn. Instead, he took the easier course of deciding that the sergeant could be conveniently transferred from the Yard to a post where a habit of loquaciousness would hardly matter.

The Midland Railway Company had applied for the 'loan' of an experienced detective who, some time in the following year, could go to them and be Superintendent of their private police. When the time came, it would be easy to promote Sergeant Meiklejohn to the rank of inspector, so that he could have the post. That would dispose of him most satisfactorily.

11

The charge of assault against Walters and Murray was not very strongly pressed, and was in due course dismissed by the magistrates. But as the two men were leaving the Court they were again arrested, and charged this time with conspiracy to defraud. Chief-Inspector Clarke would have liked more and stronger evidence against them than he had been able to collect: he would have liked it very much, because as things stood there was some chance that they might be acquitted, and then the long pursuit of them would have to begin all over again, though not until they started some fresh swindle. It was very tantalising to have them both in custody, and yet not to be certain of getting a conviction.

One day, he went to Superintendent Williamson and said, 'I've had a visit from a stockbroker, who says he has a friend, a Mr. Yonge, who is a well-to-do man living in Shanklin. Mr. Yonge, it appears, knows something about Walters and wants to tell it to me; only he is a cripple and cannot travel to London, so he wants me to go to the Isle of Wight to see him. Is there any objection to that, Mr. Williamson?'

The Superintendent would have said, 'Of course not. I don't know why you are asking me, Mr. Clarke. You know I always give my chief-inspectors a free hand——'

'Well, there's just one unusual thing about it. This Mr. Yonge wanted to give me £5 for my "expenses". I refused, of course, but it's not a proposal I like, and I don't see the reason for it, seeing that this Mr. Yonge is offering to help me, not asking me to help him. So I thought I would ask for your authority.'

'Oh, by all means go. Anything extra you can learn about Walters may be very useful.'

12

When the Chief-Inspector returned from that expedition, however, he had very little of value to report. He had not been favourably impressed by Mr. Yonge, he said: he called the man an 'infernal blackguard'. He was well-to-do, certainly—he kept a valet and a coachman, a carriage and two horses. He had once owned a newspaper in the Isle of Wight, according to what he told Clarke, but it had not been successful and he had found himself bored and wanting occupation. Then he had seen an advertisement for a skilled translator, and as he knew several languages and had plenty of spare time, he thought it would be interesting to answer it. By that means he had got into touch with Henry Walters, who needed someone to translate circulars about a betting system which were to be sent abroad. He had done the work for some time, he said, of course without any suspicion that it wasn't all fair and above board.

Superintendent Williamson would probably have said, 'Nothing very useful to you, by way of evidence against Walters, in that.'

'Oh, it wouldn't help us. As a matter of fact, though, that was what he was worrying about. He thought we might find out that he had translated the circulars and want him in the witness-box: and as he is crippled—been in a railway accident—he doesn't want to have to come to London to appear in Court. I was able to satisfy him about that—to put his mind at rest. I had to do that, though mind you I'm convinced he is a thorough scamp.'

13

Walters and Murray were duly committed for trial, bail being refused when Chief-Inspector Clarke strongly opposed it. A month later, however, a further application for bail was successful, the magistrates granting it against the wishes of the police.

Being thus set free, the two men immediately absconded and fled to America. Chief-Inspector Clarke's record of seventy-one convictions in betting swindles was not advanced that time.

CHAPTER 10

Still Easier Money

1

One day about a year later, a Mr. Abrahams, a solicitor, called at Great Scotland Yard on behalf of one of his clients, the Comtesse de Goncourt. She, he announced, had been swindled out of the sum of £10,000 by a rogue who had undertaken to assist her over betting transactions.

As he started to explain what had happened, Mr. Abrahams produced a copy of a newspaper called *The Sport.*

Chief-Inspector Clarke had seen that before.

It was not really a newspaper at all, in the ordinary sense, for although the copy bore the number 1713, to suggest that it had been published daily for several years, that was, in fact, the only issue that had ever been printed. It had the appearance of a bona-fide newspaper, with leading articles, news columns, advertisements and everything else; but nevertheless it was a complete fake. Among its articles dealing with various aspects of sport, and racing in particular, were paragraphs which drove home to its readers the news that a Mr. Hugh Montgomery had an infallible betting system.

Mr. Montgomery, the paper stated, was both the proprietor and the editor of *The Sport.* He could certainly well afford to be a newspaper owner, for he had—it was said—made a fortune of over half a million pounds by betting under his infallible system.

On one of the pages, as an item of news, was the statement that the English bookmakers had banded themselves together to boycott Mr. Montgomery, because they were all being ruined by the bets which he had placed with them under his infallible system.

Elsewhere, there was a little interesting speculation on how many months—or would it only be weeks?—it would take Mr. Montgomery to acquire another half million—under his infallible system.

And there was a leading article, written by Mr. Montgomery himself, in which he denounced as unfair the action of the bookmakers in banning his bets—because of his infallible system—and declared that he had every intention of circumventing the ban. As he could no longer place his bets himself under his own name, he was going to employ a number of agents for that purpose. By that means, he would continue, since his system was infallible, to win a fortune. The agents, however, would have to be persons residing abroad, because the rules of the Jockey Club voided any bet made in England under an assumed name or through an intermediary without disclosure of the name of the principal.[1] Mr. Montgomery was sure that many sportsmen living abroad would be glad to assist him in defeating the unfair action of the bookmakers, etc., etc., and in perpetuating the success which followed the use of his infallible system.

[1] Needless to say, that statement, like others made by Mr. Montgomery, was quite untrue.

The Comtesse de Goncourt, it appeared, had received a copy of *The Sport*, together with a translation into French of the leading article. A few days later, she received a letter, also in French, direct from Mr. Montgomery. In it he said that her name had been favourably mentioned to him by the Franco-English Society of Publicity[1] and therefore he 'reposed in her the most extreme confidence'. He accordingly begged her to assist him by acting as one of his agents in this matter, so that his bets might continue to be laid. He enclosed a cheque for £200, drawn on the Royal Bank of London,[2] and asked her to place that sum, through an English bookmaker named Jackson,[3] on a certain horse.[4] When the horse had won—as it was bound to do under Mr. Montgomery's infallible system—and she had received her winnings from the bookmaker, he would be grateful if she would be so obliging as to forward to him the amount she received. He would then appreciate her acceptance of commission on the winnings at the rate of 5 per cent.

That appeared to the Comtesse to be an admirable arrangement. As the transaction was all to be done with Mr. Montgomery's money, which he had already sent her by cheque, it would cost her nothing—and she would be the gainer by that 5 per cent commission. Really, it was quite marvellous.

Consequently, she was not at all disturbed by the fact that Mr. Montgomery requested her, 'in order to comply with the English law',[5] not to pay in the cheque for £200 until three months had passed, although any cheques

[1] There was, of course, no such society.
[2] There was, of course, no such bank.
[3] There was, of course, no such bookmaker.
[4] There was, of course, no such horse.
[5] There was, of course, no such law.

she received by way of commission could be paid in at once.

2

In due course, the Comtesse heard from the English bookmaker, Jackson, that the horse had won, and she received his cheque for her winnings. That cheque she endorsed (as she had been asked to do in the more detailed arrangements) and posted to Mr. Montgomery, who immediately sent her his cheque—not, this time, on the Royal Bank of London—for her commission.

Naturally, the Comtesse was quite willing to oblige Mr. Montgomery again, on the same terms, the next time he requested her assistance. That time, the cheque on the Royal Bank of London which she received was for £1,000, and she was asked to place it, through a bookmaker named Francis, on a horse that was running in the Great Northern Handicap.[1] This she did, and in due course the transaction was completed as before and she received her commission.

The Comtesse, of course, was tremendously impressed by those two successes which Mr. Montgomery had secured under his infallible system. She was a very wealthy woman. She could, obviously, become a still wealthier one if she did what Mr. Montgomery was doing. Why, after all, should she be content with the paltry sums she was receiving as commission for helping him, when by investing her own money—under his infallible system—she could with equal ease make thousands of pounds?

She started with a bet of £1,000. Back came a letter from the bookmaker, saying that the horse had won and enclosing a most satisfying cheque—drawn on the Royal

[1] There was, of course, no such race.

Bank of London—for her winnings. She was so delighted that she placed another bet, this time with £9,000, and wrote to tell Mr. Montgomery all about it. He replied that he was equally delighted at her success—though, of course, it could not have been otherwise under his system. He expressed great friendliness towards her and went out of his way to tell her 'in confidence' of something really quite exceptionally good. 'Never,' he said, 'will you find a similar opportunity to win an immense fortune.' He was having no hesitation, of course, in placing a large sum of his own money—a very large sum indeed—on this certainty. He suggested that she should place no less than £30,000 on it. And then, in a postscript, he added that if she found it inconvenient to produce so big a sum immediately, he would gladly advance half the amount himself for her.

Madame la Comtesse thought that most extremely obliging of Mr. Montgomery, but it was obviously worth her while to sell some of her less profitable investments in order to raise the whole of the £30,000 herself. She would do so, she declared, and would send her cheque to Mr. Montgomery—to whom she remained eternally grateful—in a few days' time.

Her Paris solicitor, however, when he heard the details of why she wanted to raise £30,000 at a few days' notice, did not think that gratitude to Mr. Hugh Montgomery was at all necessary. He pointed out to the Comtesse that she had already parted with £10,000 to a stranger in England of whom she knew nothing, and all she had had in return was a few hundred pounds as commission, plus a number of cheques of high denomination which had not been paid in and which, in any case, as he found, were drawn on a bank that didn't exist. It was obvious, he declared, that here was a swindle on a very large scale. He reported the matter to his friend and colleague, Mr. Abrahams, with the request that it should be laid before the authorities at Scotland Yard.

3

Superintendent Williamson would normally have entrusted the case, as yet another turf swindle, to Chief-Inspector Clarke. It seemed, however, that a swift pounce would secure Mr. Montgomery—or whoever was using that alias; and after that the preparation of a case against him would mainly have to be done in Paris. Clarke would not be able to do that, because he did not speak French. The warrant for Montgomery was therefore given to Chief-Inspector Druscovich.

That arrest should have gone without a hitch, since no one in England knew that the case was even in the hands of Scotland Yard except Mr. Abrahams, Superintendent Williamson, Chief-Inspector Clarke and Chief-Inspector Druscovich. Obviously, nothing could go wrong in those circumstances.

And yet Druscovich came back later in the day to report that all he had found at Mr. Montgomery's address was an empty office, locked and apparently untenanted. What was more, he had made enquiries in the neighbourhood and had learnt that the occupants had packed up and departed only an hour before his arrival.

There could be only one explanation of that.

Montgomery and his gang had a flourishing swindle on hand; they must have been waiting feverishly for the Comtesse de Goncourt's £30,000 cheque. Once they had got that, they might have thought it was wise to decamp at once, without waiting to see if they could get more still out of the credulous woman; but why on earth should they throw away that stupendous prize—unless they knew that the police were coming instead of it?

And if they knew that—if they had learnt it at the very last minute, how had the news come to them?

They might have had a spy in France who had been shadowing Madame la Comtesse, knew that she had visited her solicitor, knew that he had made enquiries about the existence of the Royal Bank of London, knew that he had written to Mr. Abrahams.

They might have had a 'contact' at Bow Street, and so have learnt of the issue of the warrant.

Otherwise, they could only have heard the news from someone at Great Scotland Yard.

The idea of a spy in France was feasible—but it certainly did not apply to all the other cases in which information had 'leaked'. The idea of a contact at Bow Street did not apply to the arrest of Henry Street, a year before, since he had been caught red-handed. No, the only possibility which fitted *all* the cases was that someone at Scotland Yard was 'talking'.

This time, moreover, it was not Sergeant Meiklejohn, for he had now been promoted inspector, had been seconded to the Midland Railway Police Force a fortnight ago, and was stationed in Derby.

It must, therefore, be one of the men whom Chief-Inspector Druscovich had taken with him to make the arrests.

And—there was really no getting away from this, now, however unpalatable it sounded—this was no matter of mere 'indiscretion'. You might talk unwisely once, or even twice: you didn't do it, by mere inadvertence, *every* time a police raid was planned, over a period of more than two years. And since the leakage was only in these turf cases, it followed that there was one man—or a central organisation—behind all the turf cases, with a 'contact' at Scotland Yard.

Moreover—since it was now necessary to face all the dreadful implications of this and not shirk any of them—nobody would become a 'contact' in that sense, and constantly betray his trust, unless it had been made 'worth his while'.

How was it possible any longer to doubt that some officer of the Detective Department was receiving *bribes*?

4

Meanwhile, whatever action might have to be taken because of that conclusion, the work of the Department had to continue. In particular, at the moment, this man Montgomery had to be traced and arrested.

It did not take long to prove that the addresses supplied to the Comtesse as those of 'English bookmakers' (Jackson, Francis and the rest) were false: or rather that they were not the addresses of genuine bookmakers, and that the persons who had answered the Comtesse's letters and had sent her bogus cheques for her 'winnings' had now, like Montgomery, decamped and gone into hiding.

The most obvious way of getting on to the trail of the gang was through Madame la Comtesse's cheques. They must have been cashed for Bank of England notes, which could be traced by their numbers.

Accordingly, Chief-Inspector Druscovich was again set to work. He returned after some days to report that he had succeeded in tracing the notes to Scotland, where they had been exchanged for Clydesdale bank-notes—doubtless for the excellent reason that the numbers on

Scottish notes were not recorded. There the trail had ended: there was no possible means by which the Clydesdale notes could be traced.

Druscovich appeared badly discouraged and inclined to think that nothing more could be done: but it was always when things were difficult that Superintendent Williamson was eager to go on. . . .

'If you've found out that much,' he would have said, 'you must have a description of the man who did the changing.'

'Yes, of course, sir. He is fairly young, a cripple, with scars on his face. I've asked round the office, but nobody can identify him.'

'Ah. A cripple? Now, where have I heard of a cripple in connection with one of these turf cases? No, that escapes me. You'll have to return to Scotland and trace the man, Mr. Druscovich. Luckily, he sounds very distinctive.'

'I'll try, sir, if you wish it, but, of course, Scotland is a very big place and I've really nothing to go on. Besides—— The case is being made extra difficult for me, sir, because that Mr. Abrahams is making enquiries on his own, with private detectives. They get in my way, and they may disclose too much. I trust, sir, that their activities can be stopped?'

Superintendent Williamson would have been disturbed by that conversation—by every part of it. Mr. Druscovich had always been an alert, exuberant man, and full of enthusiasm for his work: it was extraordinary that he should now be deterred at every check and complaining at every difficulty. It was unlike him, altogether, to be like that.

5

It would not have taken Williamson very long to remember where he had heard of a cripple in connection with turf frauds.

Nearly two years before, Mr. Clarke had gone down to Shanklin, in the Isle of Wight, to see a man who was going to give him some information about Henry Walters. Actually, there had been very little information—none of any value. But this man—what was his name? Oh yes, Yonge—had said that he had been doing some translating of the circulars into Continental languages. Of course, without any suspicion that there had been any fraud connected with them: that was what he had said to Mr. Clarke.

And hadn't Mr. Clarke described him as 'an infernal blackguard'?

That man had been a cripple—Mr. Clarke mentioned that he had been hurt in a railway accident. A cripple, working for Walters. Now, there was a cripple getting rid of the Comtesse de Goncourt's money, after a crime in which it was very likely that Walters had played a part.

Was it likely that Walters employed *two* cripples? In any case, this man Yonge had worked for Walters, on his own confession. He could therefore be charged as an accomplice: it would be for him to prove that he had done the work innocently, if he could. And if he couldn't prove that, there could be other charges. Once the man was under lock and key, a lot more could be found out about him.

6

Accordingly, when Chief-Inspector Druscovich reported that the cripple had come from Scotland to London, and that Sergeant von Tornow had been set to trace his movements beyond St. Pancras, Superintendent Williamson had a better plan fully prepared. Druscovich was to go to a house called 'Rosebank' in Shanklin, with a warrant, and arrest Mr. Yonge: he was to take with him a couple of men, who were not even to be allowed to know to what part of the country they were going, and much less who was to be arrested. In fact, this time everything was to be done under conditions of complete secrecy. . . . 'I would like to be sure that no one knows of this planned arrest except you and myself, Mr. Druscovich. I don't want there to be any mistake this time.'

Before Druscovich could complete his preparations and start, however, a telegram arrived from the Edinburgh police, reporting that they were on the track of a fresh betting swindle on much the same lines as the de Goncourt case. The implication was that the same gang was behind both cases, in which event it was likely that Yonge—if he were indeed the cripple they were looking for—would have returned to Scotland.

Superintendent Williamson therefore sent for Druscovich again and asked him how far the cripple had been traced from St. Pancras by Sergeant von Tornow. The reply was extremely unsatisfactory. The man had taken a cab, but it had 'broken down' and he had transferred himself to another. In the confusion caused by the accident the sergeant had lost sight of his quarry and had been unable to find him again. There was therefore nothing either to confirm or to deny the idea that the cripple had doubled on his tracks.

That was annoying, but there was something worse about it than mere causes for annoyance. Here was yet another case of a criminal being 'lost' by a detective.

Young Sergeant von Tornow was a nice boy, well-trained and efficient, as well as intelligent. He *couldn't*, surely, let a man he was set to follow get away from him in the middle of London—a cripple, who couldn't move very fast, moreover. . . .

Surely it didn't mean that von Tornow had put money in his own pocket, to let the man get away?

And then there was Sergeant Meiklejohn. The telegram from the Edinburgh police had given the surprising news that he was in Edinburgh. What was he doing there, just at this moment when all the principal turf swindlers seemed to be gathered in Scotland?

And there was somebody else—there must be somebody else, since there had been betrayal in cases in which neither von Tornow nor Meiklejohn had played any part.

Who was it? Who was it?

At this rate, one would come to suspecting everyone in the Department.

Probably von Tornow had only made the sort of careless mistake that any man might make occasionally. Probably Meiklejohn had legitimate business in Edinburgh, in search of goods lost or stolen on the railway. But this affair made one look at every happening with dark suspicion. For however reasonable one might try to be, the fact always remained that these turf swindlers invariably slipped away, and therefore there must be someone in the Department who was betraying even the closest secrets.

However that might be, the enquiry had still to continue. In view of the telegram from Edinburgh, valuable time might be lost if Druscovich were sent to the Isle of Wight on a gamble which might possibly produce no winnings. It would be better—probably—for him to try again in Scotland; particularly since the Scottish police had now got hold of something definite—evidence that the wanted men had recently been at an hotel at Bridge of Allan. If they could be caught there. . . .

By that time, Williamson must have been feeling that it would be a miracle if they were ever caught anywhere. Doubtless they would slip away again. Doubtless someone was listening even now to this very private conversation between himself and Mr. Druscovich—and in another minute a telegram would be sent to warn the criminals. . . . It was unbelievable. The whole thing was like a nightmare.

Nevertheless he repeated his orders to Druscovich, adding that if the gang had again slipped away he was to search the hotel most thoroughly and send to Scotland Yard—addressed to the Superintendent personally—anything connected with the men that he might find. 'Those are my orders, Mr. Druscovich. I expect you this time to effect the arrests. If—if anything goes wrong, and you are unable to do so, I require you to make that search and send me anything you find. You are to tell no one of what you are going to do before you do it. There must be complete secrecy. You quite understand? I am holding you responsible for the execution of my orders.'

7

Before long further and more definite information arrived both from the Edinburgh police and from the private detectives who (to the expressed disgust of Chief-Inspector Druscovich) were still making enquiries on behalf of Mr. Abrahams. Through these two sources it was established definitely that the cripple was the Mr. Yonge of Shanklin, and that another of the criminals was known as Gifford. Both these men had recently been seen in the Queen's Hotel, Bridge of Allan.

The only thing now needed, therefore, was the arrival of Druscovich with the warrants: that, and the 'miracle' which would enable them to be executed before the criminals learnt what was on foot and decamped.

8

Of course, the question—if it *was* still a 'question'—of whether someone in the Department was being bribed had long ago been fully reported by the Superintendent to the Commissioner and was thus largely out of Williamson's hands.

Indeed, it was largely out of Colonel Henderson's hands as well, for he had reported the matter to the Home Secretary, and the Treasury Solicitor had started a secret enquiry.

Accordingly, down through the hierarchy of officials, Williamson received orders to write formally to demand reports and explanations from Inspector Meiklejohn—and from Chief-Inspector Druscovich, whose quarries always 'got away'.

By that time, there seemed the most definite reasons for suspecting Meiklejohn of conspiring with the criminals; and accordingly Williamson's letter stated:

'A statement has been made to the Commissioner that from the 4th to the 6th instant you were at the Queen's Hotel, Bridge of Allan, in company with two men named Yonge and Gifford, who are wanted for committing extensive frauds. Yonge is said to have lodged with you. You are to report in explanation.'

To this Meiklejohn replied that, while enquiring after a stolen portmanteau, he had met Mr. Yonge, a well-to-do man from whom he had once received some useful information. Mr. Yonge had been accompanied by a friend whom Meiklejohn did not know. Not being at the Yard now, he had, of course, no knowledge of warrants and had had no reason to suspect that Mr. Yonge and his friend were anything but honest men.

The letter to Druscovich could not, naturally, be anything like so definite as that to Meiklejohn: and indeed it is doubtful whether Williamson would have cared to make what would look like an accusation against one of his trusted chief-inspectors. He had, however, to ask for 'explanations'.

He received a very prompt reply. Druscovich professed ignorance, apologetically, as to what he was asked to report on and what he was required to explain. It was unfortunate indeed that the criminals had slipped through the nets he had carefully laid for them, but they were very elusive characters and the pursuit had therefore been extremely difficult. But he would be grateful if the Superintendent would kindly convey to the Commissioner his assurance that every endeavour was being made to effect the arrests as soon as possible.

Thus Inspector Meiklejohn had an explanation, and Chief-Inspector Druscovich felt he had nothing to explain.

CHAPTER 11

Proof of Guilt

1

Superintendent Williamson can hardly have been surprised—though he must have been still more intensely worried—when a telegram came from Druscovich in Scotland, saying that the men he was after had disappeared 'into thin air' shortly before his arrival.

It was becoming difficult to remember when Druscovich had succeeded in any mission entrusted to him . . . certainly, when he was sent to arrest any member of a turf gang, the criminal always got away.

That undeniable fact made the Chief-Inspector's enquiry about 'What had he to explain?' look extremely specious. Yet surely it wasn't possible to believe that one of the Department's three chief-inspectors—whom Williamson had always regarded as men of complete integrity and loyalty—could be a traitor—a traitor in receipt of bribes?

2

There was, however, the fact that Druscovich was now definitely disobeying his orders—or pretending that he

CHIEF-INSPECTOR NAT. DRUSCOVICH

"Smart in appearance as well as in character"

had forgotten them. He had not been told to send telegrams reporting failure: the orders had been that in the event of failure he was to take other steps immediately—the searching of the hotel at Bridge of Allan and the production of anything he found there.

Williamson therefore wired somewhat peremptorily to Druscovich, demanding the results of that search. After all, if the criminals had practically walked out of the back door as the police came in at the front, as seemed to have been the case, it was highly probable that in their hurry they would have left something behind.

That telegram left no loophole for Druscovich: coming as it did just after the formal demand for 'explanations', it showed very clearly that the authorities at Scotland Yard had got beyond the point when they could be put off by evasions.

Consequently, there soon arrived on Superintendent Williamson's desk an envelope marked 'Private and Personal'.

In it were three enclosures.

The first was a piece of blotting-paper. Written on it, in printed characters which could not be identified as any one person's hand-writing, were the words: '*Keep the lame man out of the way.*'

Williamson's fingers must have trembled as he read it. 'The lame man'—that would be Yonge, of course. He was to be hidden from the police—the warning could mean nothing else. It could only have come from someone who knew that Yonge was in danger of arrest. Moreover, the blotting paper was of the type which was used at Scotland Yard.

Oh yes, yes. It was proof positive that someone in the Department was in league with these swindlers.

But who? There was no indication, in those printed capitals. . . .

The next paper was a telegram:

W. Gifford, Queen's Hotel, Bridge of Allan, Scotland.

If Shanks is near the Isle of Wight let him leave at once and see you—letter follows.

W. Brown, London.

And finally there was a letter, also to W. Gifford:

There is very strong particulars from Edinburgh, which I suppose you know; they have the address at the shop here. It is also known that you were in Edinburgh a day or two ago. Perhaps you had better see me—things begin to look fishy. News may be given to the Isle of Wight, where Shanklin is. You know best. D goes to the Isle of Wight tomorrow. Send this back.

W. Brown, who was with you at the 'Daniel Lambert'.

Williamson must have stared at that letter in utter surprise and dismay. For although, at the beginning, there had apparently been some attempt to disguise the hand-writing, that had faded out as the letter progressed. It was, without question, the hand-writing of Chief-Inspector Palmer.

3

Williamson had never for one moment suspected Palmer. He was, indeed, the very last person—well, the last but one, because no one could ever suspect George Clarke—whom one could suspect: a man incapable of any

CHIEF-INSPECTOR WILLIAM PALMER

"The solid, perhaps stolid, type"

underhand action, a man with an essentially British sense of loyalty. At least, that was how Williamson had always thought of him till this moment.

Yet there was no getting away from the evidence of that letter. Palmer's hand-writing was quite distinctive, there was no mistaking it. It was thus clearly established that Palmer had been in communication, under the assumed name of W. Brown, with one of the criminals at the Bridge of Allan.

The wording of that letter revealed many things. '*Perhaps you had better see me . . . You know best.*' Those words implied that the two men knew each other, were accustomed to work together. And '*Send this back*'—a clear admission that the writer knew his guilt and the danger of what he was doing.

And then, '*D goes to the Isle of Wight tomorrow.*' 'D' was Druscovich, of course. But Gifford would not have known whom the initial stood for unless there had been previous communications.

No, it was now clear—horribly, painfully clear—that for months if not for years Palmer had been hand in glove with these swindlers. It was through his secret warnings that so many of them had repeatedly escaped.

4

There was that line in Palmer's letter—'*D goes to the Isle of Wight tomorrow.*' Druscovich had never gone to the Isle of Wight: those orders had been countermanded within a few hours of their being given. They had been given, moreover, under conditions of absolute secrecy, and Druscovich had been specially warned that no one was to know of the plan. No one *had* known of it except

Williamson and Druscovich. And yet, in those few hours between the giving of the orders and the countermanding of them, William Palmer had been able to send that telegram of warning and to write that letter!

How had he known of the orders? How could he possibly have known—unless Druscovich, in direct defiance of what he had been ordered a few minutes before, had passed on the information?

And why should Druscovich have done such a thing? Would a responsible chief-inspector gossip innocently to a friend when he had been specifically told not to do anything of the sort? No, no, the idea was absurd—utterly absurd, when taken in conjunction with the suspicions which already existed against Druscovich, and the fact of his repeated failures to make arrests. He must have passed the news to Palmer, knowing that Palmer would at once send telegrams and letters. In other words, Druscovich, as well as Palmer, must be in the pay of the criminals.

But in that case, why had Druscovich forwarded the papers found at the Bridge of Allan Hotel? Not, certainly, because of an instinct to obey orders! Nor out of any guileless thinking that they wouldn't be understood, or that the hand-writing of the letter would not be recognised. No. There had been that official demand for 'explanations', a doubt whether the bland reply, 'What have I to explain?' had produced any good results, and finally Williamson's peremptory telegram to show that it had not and that the old relationship of trust and friendship had been replaced by dark suspicion. Druscovich then must have seen the net closing around him; and as a last desperate turn he must have decided to disclose the evidence against Palmer. No doubt he had imagined—or at any rate hoped—that once there was definite evidence against one culprit, there would be no further enquiries, and the other culprit—he himself—would go free.

5

The next few days must have been days of torment to Superintendent Williamson. He had of course reported the whole matter to the Commissioner, and had handed over Palmer's telegram and the letter and the scrap of blotting-paper. Then he was told that as the matter was in the hands of the Treasury solicitor, nothing could be done until orders were received 'from higher authority'. Druscovich and Palmer could not be suspended, they must continue at their work, and no hint might be given to them or to anyone of what was suspected. But at the same time, it would be most unwise—unsafe, indeed—to trust either of them with any secrets.

In that predicament, Superintendent Williamson did the only thing he could do. He took the whole work of the Department into his own hands, trusting no one except Chief-Inspector Clarke. It meant working sixteen hours a day. It involved the embarrassment of deflecting work that would normally have gone to Palmer and Druscovich—that hardly came strictly under the heading of 'giving no hint', but then he had received contradictory orders, to 'give no hint' and to 'show no trust' and he could not do both of those things. In any case, the safety and honour of the Department always came first in his mind.

6

The members of the gang were gradually being identified. Yonge was a man named Benson, who had once tried to commit suicide in prison by setting fire to his bed—his scars and limp were the result of that, and not, as he had told Chief-Inspector Clarke, of a railway accident. 'W. Gifford', to whom Palmer had written, was William Kurr. Edwin Murray, who had returned from America after absconding with Henry Walters from his bail in an earlier case, was in the gang, together with 'Jerry the Greengrocer' and others who were well-known to the police. Well-known, but not yet caught. It was very difficult to catch anyone when the detectives sent after them could not be trusted.

Chief-Inspector Clarke came to Williamson one day and said, 'There's a rat named Savory come to see me. Unsavoury is what I'd call him. He is something to do with the de Goncourt gang: on the fringe of it, anyway. Edwin Murray wants him to change some of those Clydesdale notes, and he doesn't like Murray very much, so he thinks it would be a nice idea if I went along with him to a meeting he has fixed with Murray at Charing Cross Station tonight. It might be a good idea if I went, Mr. Williamson. I don't like Murray very much either.'

Williamson agreed. Though Murray was not the biggest man in the gang, it would be something to secure him—if it could be done. There would, of course, be no betrayal if the arrest was handled by Clarke himself, but there would have to be exceptional care that no one else knew in advance of what was to happen. . . .

That, at any rate, was accomplished successfully. There, then, was one of the gang locked up. The others appeared to have scattered and gone into hiding. A watch was being kept on William Kurr's house in London, but he never came near it. Harry Benson never went near the house in Shanklin in which he had lived (with a coachman and a valet, and a carriage and pair) as 'G. H. Yonge'. Once again, all the trails had faded out.

7

A telegram came from the police at Rotterdam. It reported that three Englishmen, staying there, had attempted to pay their hotel bill with a Clydesdale note. The hotel-keeper had been suspicious and had reported the matter to the police, and the three men had been detained.

Ordinarily, in a matter that called first for indentification and then for extradition proceedings, Chief-Inspector Druscovich would have been sent abroad to deal with it. But that, of course, was out of the question now. Superintendent Williamson went, himself, to Rotterdam.

The three men proved to be Benson and two others of the gang. Williamson had no difficulty in identifying them, from descriptions supplied to him by Chief-Inspector Clarke; but if further confirmation had been needed, it had been supplied in a way that went far to help the extradition proceedings. Just before Williamson's arrival, the Dutch police had received a telegram which purported to come from Scotland Yard and said that the three arrested men were not those the English police were seeking and should therefore be set free! Luckily, William Kurr—for no one else could have forged that telegram—had added 'letter follows' and the Rotterdam police had accordingly decided to take no action till they had fuller information.

The extradition proceedings went through quickly. So did the subsequent trials. In due course, Harry Benson, alias Yonge, was sentenced, on a charge of conspiracy to defraud, to penal servitude for 15 years. Three others (including William Kurr) received 10 years each, and Edwin Murray, as an accessory after the fact, was sentenced to 18 months hard labour.

8

Thus the series of turf frauds came at last to an end. . . .

But the crisis at Scotland Yard continued. On the surface, it looked as if that too had reached its end; for the Treasury solicitor, after very fully considering the matter, decided that it would be unwise to bring prosecutions. Against Druscovich and Meiklejohn there was very little actual evidence of the kind that would convince a jury of their guilt: it was all very well for Superintendent Williamson to suspect, and for the Commissioner to feel sure—but even they, if they had been on the jury, might have hesitated. There was certainly no legal proof.

Against Palmer there was tangible evidence, certainly; but it was considered impracticable to charge him without charging the other two as well. And if—whatever happened to Palmer—the others were aquitted, a most undesirable situation would be created. The Crown would have charged two of its own most valued servants with disgraceful crime, and they would have been found to be innocent men! The public scandal would be terrific.

So nothing was to be done. Inspector Meiklejohn was to continue looking for stolen portmanteaux from his office in Derby. Chief-Inspectors Palmer and Druscovich were to continue in their positions in the Detective Department at Great Scotland Yard, doing their ordinary work. . . .

Only, of course, as Colonel Henderson warned Superintendent Williamson, it would still be most unwise to trust either of them with any secret information.

9

And then, only a few months later, the whole situation changed. Williamson was sent for by the Commissioner and told that prosecutions against all the three men were to be started immediately: they were to be charged with 'conspiring with William Kurr and others to obstruct, defeat and pervert the due course of public justice'.

Williamson must have stared in astonishment at the Commissioner as he heard those words.

'But—but you told me, sir——'

'I told you the Home Secretary's decision of ten weeks ago. The position now is radically altered. Yonge and Kurr and the others have turned Queen's evidence, and have made full statements declaring that they gave substantial bribes to each of the three officers. Here are the warrants. You will make the arrests without any delay.'

CHAPTER 12

Scenes in Court

1

The police-court proceedings against Palmer, Druscovich and Meiklejohn opened at Bow Street. Superintendent Williamson had to be in Court every day, to give evidence of the arrests and on other points and to 'keep a watch on the case'. There was a fourth prisoner in the dock, a solicitor named Froggart. Frederick Williamson would not have been interested in him: but the sight of Chief-Inspector Palmer, Chief-Inspector Druscovich and Inspector Meiklejohn ('three of the best-known officers in the Detective Department', as *The Times* called them), in that situation, would have been like a scene in a nightmare to him.

It must be assumed that he had never completely made up his mind about their guilt; that all along, as the suspicion grew, he had fought against it—chiefly because he did not like it. He had always had that sense of close friendship for the men with whom he worked: and he was always loyal to friendship.

But now he had to sit and listen as William Kurr gave his evidence and unfolded a tale of perfidy on the part of the police which could not be heard without a shudder.

Of course, it might not be true. Why should anyone believe the word of such a scoundrel as William Kurr, who certainly would not hesitate to perjure himself in the witness box, if he thought that by doing so he might secure some remission of his own sentence? And yet—there was the undeniable fact that what he said fitted in remarkably closely—terribly closely—with all that Williamson had himself suspected. And, more than that, what he said explained categorically every one of the recent failures in making arrests.

2

Kurr said that he had known Meiklejohn for the last five years, and that the inspector, in the days when he was a sergeant as well as more recently, had helped him all the time, in return for payments.

'In the month of June, 1874,' he said, 'I paid Meiklejohn £200 in all. That was for giving me information when I was in Glasgow. . . . In November I paid Meiklejohn £500, after first offering him £300, which he said was not enough.' The £500 had been in payment for a warning that a warrant had been issued.

The story that Kurr told about Druscovich was, if possible, even worse, though that treachery had only lasted for about eighteen months. Druscovich, it appeared, had backed a bill for his brother, and then had had to find £60 to meet it. He had asked Meiklejohn for a loan (in spite of the rule at Scotland Yard that no officer might borrow money from another officer inferior to himself in rank) and Meiklejohn had said he couldn't do it, but

'Bill Kurr would'. Druscovich, according to Kurr, had then said,[1] 'Will he keep his mouth shut?' and Meiklejohn had answered, 'Oh yes: I always go to him when I want money.' So there had been a secret meeting at Blackfriars Station, when Kurr handed Druscovich six £10 notes.

That was only the beginning. Four months later, Kurr met Druscovich again, told him something of the swindle which led to the de Goncourt case, and asked him to give warning when there were complaints, or if a warrant was issued. For that, Druscovich was given £25 in gold 'in a little bag'. Later, he was paid £500, which was left at his house in a cigar box, while Meiklejohn had a further £200, handed to his wife, in another cigar box.

There were even worse accusations. Druscovich, according to Kurr, had become afraid of being suspected at Great Scotland Yard and had refused to have any more secret meetings. And Kurr, on hearing of this, had said to Meiklejohn, 'Tell him to make all his business known at the Office. *I am sure to know, then, from others.*'

Others? Quite distinctly, there had been an 's' at the end of the word. Did it mean, then, that there had been someone besides William Palmer who was sending telegrams and messages?

Curiously, there was, as yet, no suggestion from Kurr that any money had ever been paid to Palmer: but on the other hand, Kurr spoke boastfully, and more than once, as if *everyone* at Scotland Yard was in his pay. Or at least, almost everyone. Once, Kurr had said to Meiklejohn, 'Well, don't you think Mr. Williamson will be suspicious about this?' And Meiklejohn had answered, 'Oh, he's a calf. He will never tumble to it in a thousand years.'

[1] This evidence, of course, should hardly have been admitted, since Kurr was only repeating what Meiklejohn had told him.

Williamson had been regarded as incorruptible. But few other men came into that category. Kurr said that he and his gang had bribed 'the police in Scotland Yard and America, the warders in Newgate, in the House of Detention and at Millbank', as well as two Post Office Inspectors and an Inspector of the City Police, 'and a good many more'. Specifically, among the Scotland Yard officers, he named Sergeant von Tornow, who failed to keep track of Benson when a cab broke down in the streets of London: 'I had a conversation with von Tornow and gave him £10 in a public house.'

3

Only one of those somewhat wholesale accusations was considered seriously, at that time, by the authorities: that was the one against von Tornow. That, probably, would have been passed as mere boastfulness on Kurr's part, but for the fact that von Tornow lost his head when he heard of it, fled to his mother's home in Germany and wrote from there to resign from the Force.

That, of course, could not be permitted, and the boy was brought back to England. There, he had no difficulty in proving that on the date when Kurr claimed to have given him £10 at Euston he had been in Whitechapel, working on a case with another sergeant.

4

To Frederick Williamson, anxious as he was to disbelieve what was obviously the truth, the part of the story which related to von Tornow must have brought some little comfort. That accusation was palpably untrue, and proved to be untrue: why, then, should not other accusations be untrue also?

And yet—being a very human personality, he must by this time have been a little less anxious to defend these men in his mind than he had been at the start of the trial. Meiklejohn had spoken disparagingly, even sneeringly, of him, calling him 'a calf'. Druscovich had treated him like a child to be humoured, asking 'What is there to explain?' And Palmer—well, of Palmer's guilt there was no possible doubt, after his letter signed 'W. Brown' and his 'Send this back'. All three of them had not only betrayed the Department, they had also treated Williamson himself with contempt. He must have realised, with great bitterness, that they had laughed about him, amongst themselves and with the criminals who paid them.

Thus he would have been torn between two ideas, his bitterness at what had happened and his memory of old friendships. Probably, in the inevitable outcome of the trial, the bitterness would have prevented the shattering of memories from being too painful.

But then——there came a day when William Kurr was under cross-examination by Counsel for the various defendants. Mr. Montague Williams, as Counsel for Meiklejohn, started off by saying, 'Give me the names of the police connected with this case to whom you say you have given bribes.' And Kurr answered, 'I have given bribes to Meiklejohn and Druscovich. Indirectly, I have also given them to Palmer and von Tornow—and to Chief-Inspector Clarke.'

Frederick Williamson must have felt like jumping to his feet and crying out that that was a lie. Of course it was a lie. Whatever Palmer and Druscovich and Meiklejohn might do, George Clarke was a completely honest man, and open and loyal and dependable. And—something more than that: a man you trusted as you only trust a close friend. It was a ridiculous lie to say he had taken a bribe.

Of course, the lie would be nailed down as the one about von Tornow had been nailed down. . . .

Counsel was saying, 'Then at the moment I will ask you about the amount you gave to Chief-Inspector Clarke.'

Kurr said, 'About £200. I gave him £50 in August, and on the day Benson returned from Scotland I gave him indirectly £150.'

'That is all you have ever given him?'

'Oh no. In the case of Walters and Murray, about the middle of August, 1875, I gave him two £50 notes.'

' "Directly" or "indirectly"?'

'Direct, in that case.'

'And what do you mean by "indirectly"?'

'When I don't hand it over myself, but give it through someone else. I gave Clarke the £150 through Benson.'

'You mean,' said Counsel, 'that you gave Benson £150 to give to Clarke. Have you any acknowledgment? Any evidence that Clarke received it?'

'Oh, he got it all right,' Kurr answered. 'I know that, because of the things he did in return for it.'

5

So definite an accusation, in public Court, could not possibly have been hushed up. From the way the newspapers printed the news, it was obvious that they expected Chief-Inspector Clarke to be arrested and put to stand his trial with the others.

And indeed, no one—except, as we may suppose, Frederick Williamson—wanted it to be 'hushed up'. The view in high places was that as the matter had been brought out into the open, the consequences must be faced and all accusations must be met. The jury alone could decide whether such accusations were justified.

At that stage, then, Clarke was ordered to make a report. He did so, at considerable length. He denied emphatically that he had ever taken bribes. But at the same time he admitted things which had never been told to anyone before. . . .

Apart from that formal report, he had, of course, now talked about the situation to Williamson. We know that, from Williamson's own evidence at the trial: 'Clarke . . . did not tell me about that till after his case had commenced. He then told me . . .' Williamson gave no full account of what Clarke said to him, in what must have been an extremely distressing and embarrassing talk, but it is obvious that it must have been very closely on the lines of what was written in his report. . . .

'You see, when I was handling that burglary at Stannard's Mill, in Essex,[1] I was pretty sure I could get some useful information out of Henry Walters.'

'Yes, yes. I remember you saying you wished you could get him to talk, and that you thought of writing to him. Go on, go on.'

'Well, I wrote him a note, asking him to meet me. Seemed the best way to do things. I asked him to call at my house in the evening if he could, or to meet me at Charing Cross the next day, if that was better. Nothing in that, of course, nothing at all. The sort of thing we often do, isn't it? Only perhaps I didn't word the letter as

[1] See *ante*, p. 125.

carefully as I might have done—I put in a bit about "Don't show this or bring anyone with you", because, you see, I was going to ask him to betray his pals, and that's a thing that is better not talked about, or known about.'

'Of course. That's reasonable enough. But—what happened?'

'Nothing, until some time later when I got that request that I should go and see Yonge—Benson, as we now know him to be—in Shanklin. You'll remember that I couldn't make out why he offered to pay my expenses, seeing that the trip was for my advantage, not his. Or so it seemed. And I got your authority——'

'Yes, yes. Go on.'

'Well, what happened at Shanklin was what I told you, up to a point. There was more that I didn't tell you, didn't tell anyone.'

Frederick Williamson must have been aghast at that. George Clarke was admitting that—at least—he had falsified reports. It was unbelievable! And yet, perhaps after all it wasn't quite as bad as that. There was a rule that chief-inspectors reported results, not the steps they took before anything happened. If this was no more than that. . . .

'I always say nobody can catch me,' Clarke would have gone on. 'But Benson caught me, that time. Benson and Walters between them, I suppose. Benson told me that Walters had told him that at that meeting he had offered me a bribe. And he said Walters had kept my letter—with the bit in it about not showing it to anyone—as a proof that I'd had secret negotiations with him and—well, had taken money from him. Of course, that was a lie. On my honour, I never took money from anyone. Not a penny.'

'You didn't tell me this before. Why didn't you? If there was nothing in it——'

'Didn't know what you'd think. Y'see, when Benson put it like that, I saw that my letter *could* be read as if it meant something nasty, like he said. And—well, I ought to have come to you, I see that now. Only—you see, the suggestion was that Walters would send my letter to the Commissioner, with his explanation of what it meant and the flat statement that I had taken money from him. So I thought I'd better get the letter back first, and report afterwards. Benson said he'd try to get it for me; but, of course, that was all part of the trick. What Benson was after——'

'Yes? Yes? You were being blackmailed, obviously. What was the idea of that?'

'They wanted from me what Mr. Druscovich and the others gave them. Information and tipping-off. There's been a lot of pressure put on me. I'd be quite a rich man, if I'd taken all they offered me.'

6

Kurr continued to make definite accusations. 'When I handed Clarke the £50 in August,' he declared, 'he said, all in one breath, "You can't afford that—thanks", and put the money in his pocket.'

Benson, when he went into the witness-box, had also much to say on the subject. 'I gave Clarke £50 in gold . . . I saw Clarke again, when I gave him £50 in notes.'

Thus it was inevitable that, a fortnight before the Bow Street proceedings ended in a committal for trial, Chief-Inspector Clarke appeared in the dock, alongside Chief-

Inspector Druscovich, Chief-Inspector Palmer and Inspector Meiklejohn. All three of the most senior officers of the Detective Department, under Superintendent Williamson, were now accused together.

7

At the Old Bailey, there were still further accusations against Clarke.

There was an amazing story of how he had been given a number of envelopes addressed to William Kurr and told that if he posted one of them, with nothing in it but a blank sheet of paper—thus avoiding the risk to himself involved in writing anything—Kurr would at once come and see him at his home; and that Clarke had agreed to that scheme, and consequently had been paid £50 'in consideration of future services'.

There was the point made very strongly by the Attorney General that the letter to Walters—the subject of the alleged blackmailing—had contained neither address nor signature: and yet the suggestion, 'I shall be glad if you will make it convenient to call at my house', was meant to be, and assumed to be, intelligible to the recipient. How, demanded the Attorney General, was that possible, unless there had been previous correspondence, so that Walters knew the identity of the writer from the handwriting? And how would Walters have known where to go, if there had not been previous secret meetings?

Benson declared that Clarke had concocted a scheme to prevent anyone arresting Edwin Murray without his sanction, which he agreed not to give. Kurr claimed that he had met Clarke secretly no less than ten times: and that once Clarke had boasted to him that he had had an opportunity to arrest Henry Walters, but had deliberately allowed him to escape. And Kurr also declared that Clarke had said that it was he who had written the message on blotting-paper—'Keep the lame man out of the way.'

8

As the case drew to its close, there was not very much that the various Counsel could say in defence of men who seemed obviously guilty.

The chief claim on behalf of Meiklejohn was that everything depended on the stories of Kurr and Benson, and if those stories were found untrue in some respects, then they could not be trusted in other respects. 'The story of the convicts is true with regard to all the defendants or none of them.' Charges had been made, not only against Meiklejohn, Druscovich and Palmer, but also against Chief-Inspector Clarke. 'Do the jury believe that a man like Clarke, with his character, antecedents and the position he has occupied for thirty-five years, would be guilty of this fraud? But if Clarke is innocent, then you cannot believe the stories of Benson and Kurr, who say that Clarke is guilty: and if you do not believe those stories, then you must also find Meiklejohn innocent.'

It was, perhaps, rather a curious argument, and not a very strong one.

Counsel for Druscovich admitted the original payment of £60 to him, but called it a loan. At the end of his speech, he implored the jury 'not to sacrifice a comparatively young life, hitherto distinguished for industry, energy and integrity, upon the evidence of two of the deepest-dyed scoundrels that ever scandalised the witness-box of a court of justice, or ever insulted the Sacred Book with kisses of lips framed only to perjury and fraud'.

A slightly more effective plea for Druscovich was given —as it happened—by the Attorney General: 'I am sorry for him, because I feel that up to a certain time he did his duty honestly and well. I am sorry for him, because he did come into the toils of the conspirators through a cruel necessity in which he found himself. He borrowed £60, and that placed him in the power of these men, and he was lured and tempted on to betray his trust and neglect his duty. But do not let any sympathy you may have with Druscovich stand between you and your duty.'

The most that could be said on behalf of Palmer was that there was no definite accusation of bribery. He 'is believed to have written the letter and telegram at the bidding of some more dominant mind, and to have kept silence rather than betray a colleague'.[1] But his counsel had very little that was effective to say for him: only vague suggestions that 'there are hand-writings which closely resemble each other', and a still vaguer suggestion that someone 'hanging around the purlieus of Old Jewry' might have happened to use the name Palmer—in fact that it might all be a case of mistaken identity.

9

There was, however, more that could be said—and was said—for Clarke. Evidence on his behalf had been given by Colonel Henderson, the Commissioner of Police ('I have found him thoroughly trustworthy'), by Superintendent Williamson ('I have never had the slightest reason to suspect him'), by Inspector Shore and four of the sergeants.

[1] Frank Dilnot.

On that basis, his Counsel said: 'Over seventy persons now look back upon their convictions, and know it was Inspector Clarke who brought them to justice. This man must have had enormous opportunities. Swindlers such as he has dealt with, getting their hundreds and thousands in a few weeks—what to them would have been a gift of money to buy his energies off? If he had been a dishonest man, do you doubt that he might have filled his hands with gold?[1] . . . Gentlemen, I do hope confidently that Clarke may go out from this court, not discharged because a jury could not agree; not with some bastard verdict of Not Proven, to hang round his neck for the rest of his life the irrevocable stigma of crime; but with the straightforward, honest "Not guilty" that will send him back to his friends an honoured man.'

10

In the end, John Meiklejohn, Nathaniel Druscovich, William Palmer and the solicitor were all found guilty: each of them was sentenced 'to be imprisoned and kept at hard labour for the period of two years', the judge expressing his regret (in spite of recommendations to mercy, by the jury, in the case of Druscovich and Palmer) that the law did not allow him to pass heavier sentences.[2]

George Clarke was acquitted.

[1] It had been said that Clarke lived in 'a little house' for which he paid a rental of £36 per annum and 'the income he derived did not permit him to occupy that house by himself. The £36 had to be paid with the assistance of lodgers.' A Chief-Inspector's salary was then only £276 a year.

[2] On being released from prison, Meiklejohn set up as a private enquiry agent, and later tried his hand at journalism. Druscovich's health broke down in prison, and he died soon after his release. Palmer became a publican.

11

There is a maxim that one should not go behind the verdict of a jury. Nevertheless, it must be said that no one—except George Clarke, Harry Benson and William Kurr—has ever known exactly how far Clarke went while he was squirming on the blackmailers' hook. He owned to being 'indiscreet' in keeping up an association with the criminals, not for purposes of his duty, but in the hope of recovering that incriminating letter. He owned to writing further letters and having secret meetings. He owned to being offered money, in attempts to suborn him from his duty. But he owned to nothing more than indiscretion, maintaining that he had remained an honest and honourable man, stoutly resisting all temptations and all threats.

It could very well be that Benson and Kurr had tried to suborn Clarke, because he could have been very useful to them—that they had eventually realised that that attempt would fail—and that then they had decided to do what would now-a-days be called 'framing' him: being all the more inclined to do that because, if he wouldn't walk with them, he was a menace to them, as indeed he had been for many years.

It may be assumed that that was the conclusion to which the jury came, even if their emotions were also swayed in his favour by his counsel's impassioned address. . . .

The matter could be left at that, but for two facts. One is that his Counsel[1] declared afterwards, 'It would have been practically impossible to obtain an acquittal if at that time the law had permitted accused persons to be

[1] It was a coincidence that George Clarke was defended by Mr. (afterwards Sir) Edward Clarke.

called as witnesses': a statement which seems to imply that Clarke's own Counsel did not believe him innocent and considered that he would have admitted his guilt under cross-examination. The other fact is that, even after the acquittal, the Police Authorities would not allow Clarke to remain in the Force.

According to *The Times* of December 15th, 1877 (three weeks after the end of the trial), 'Mr. Chief-Inspector Clarke of the Detective Department, Scotland Yard, has been reinstated on full pay. This act of the Commissioner's will entitle Mr. Clarke to the arrears of his pay since the date of his arrest, and to his full pension, on which, it is believed, he will immediately retire.' And after a further three and a half weeks, 'It is announced that Chief-Inspector Clarke has retired on a pension of £185 a year.'

Thus there were no longer any Chief-Inspectors in the Detective Department. Its staff consisted solely of Superintendent Williamson, two inspectors and a number of sergeants. Had not Williamson been an immense tower of strength in himself, the Department would have been as weak as it was ten years before. And although Williamson could do much, he could not do everything by himself. He must have found it very difficult to see how the Department could possibly be built up to its former efficiency.

PART FOUR

Sequel to The Second Crisis

CHAPTER 13

C.I.D.

1

Colonel Henderson said in his report on the work of the Metropolitan Police for the year 1877:

'The reorganisation of the Detective Department was rendered necessary during the year, consequent on the conviction of three of the principal officers for more or less complicity in an extensive case of turf fraud; and, subsequent to the period for which this report is compiled, a committee appointed by the Secretary of State for the Home Department has made a careful investigation into the whole question of the detection of crime. In accordance with their recommendations, the Detective Department has been entirely reorganised.

'It formerly consisted of about thirty officers under a Superintendent stationed at Scotland Yard . . . The divisional detectives were selected by the divisional Superintendents and employed in their own divisions. . . .

'Under the new arrangements, the Detective Department has been formed into one division, in charge of the Director of Criminal Investigations.'

2

That report was not issued until September, 1878. Five months earlier, the new arrangements had been officially described in greater detail:

'*Criminal Investigation Department.* From Monday next, April 8th, the whole of the detective establishment will form one body under the Director of Criminal Investigation. With the exception of the undermentioned officers, promoted or appointed to responsible posts, the present staff will be placed on probation for three months. . . .'

The 'establishment' was detailed as consisting of a Central Office staffed by 1 Chief-Superintendent, 3 Chief-Inspectors, 3 1st-class inspectors and 17 2nd-class inspectors, with a clerical staff of 4 sergeants and 2 constables; while there were also to be 14 'local inspectors',[1] with a force of about 200 sergeants and detective-constables, in the divisions.

'. . . The following promotions and appointments will take effect from the 8th inst. Central Office, Superintendent Williamson to be Chief-Superintendent; Detective-Inspector Shore to be Chief-Inspector. . . .'

3

Thus the arrangements for the new organisation moved very cautiously. Out of the whole of the detective force, only 14 men (because two of the divisions were left at the

[1] The list of 'local inspectors' then appointed includes Inspector Jones (T Division), Inspector O'Callaghan (N Division) and Inspector Abberline (H Division), who will figure in the later pages of this chronicle. It also includes Inspector Hagen, who was almost immediately transferred to the Central Office and later became Chief-Inspector.

start without inspectors) were regarded as unquestionably trustworthy. Of the old Detective Department at Scotland Yard (now to be the Central Office of the Criminal Investigation Department) there were only two men—Williamson and Shore—who were 'appointed' instead of being 'put on probation'. That left 2 Chief-Inspectors and 20 inspectors to be found: and not only to be found but to be tested and proved worthy. It was, indeed, a slow and careful process. Thirteen out of the twenty inspectors were appointed (mostly by promotion of sergeants) almost at once: and so good was the process of hand-picking that all except two of them were still on the strength eight years later. The selection of Chief-Inspectors was, if anything, even more exacting—as was perhaps natural, after what had happened in that rank before: for three years the whole burden of that rank was borne by Chief-Inspector Shore, alone.

4

The 'Director of Criminal Investigations' was Mr. C. E. Howard Vincent. He was an ambitious young man who made a study of the detective system at the Paris Sureté, and had written a report on it which was of value to the Home Secretary's committee. Consequently, he received the appointment to the new post.

He was, of course, an 'amateur' in detection, and a theorist: and his theories were not of British origin. In his earliest days, that brought him into trouble.

'The Superintendents of the Metropolitan Police recently presented a complaint,' announced *The Times* on October 7th, 1878, 'against the manner in which detective-constables and plainclothes officers under them were taken out of their control by the Director of the Criminal Investigation Department, the Superintendents being entirely set aside and the detectives set to work by a system of espionage, similar to that of the French secret police.

'The Superintendents having intimated that they would not be responsible for the tracing of criminals in their districts, the following memorandum has been issued from Scotland Yard to each of the Superintendents: "By order of the Commissioner, from and after the 1st prox. I shall transact the criminal business through you. It was entirely contrary to my intention to deprive myself of the great benefit of your experience. . . ." '[1]

5

It is extremely probable that Superintendent Williamson sympathised with the Divisional Superintendents in that matter. It has been said of him[2] that 'He had no faith in new departures, and, himself a police officer for nearly forty years, he regarded with the utmost distrust anyone who, not having been trained at Scotland Yard, imagined he might be of service to the authorities.' Similarly, Inspector Lansdowne described him as 'slow to grasp a new idea, doubtful of its efficacy, seeing its disadvantages rather than its advantages'.

But outside his innate points of character, Williamson was at this time a changing man.

The 'Dolly' Williamson who had enjoyed 'barneys' had died in the downfall of Jonathan Whicher. The Frederick

[1] Something of Mr. Howard Vincent's character may be gathered from the extreme tact of this remark, together with the fact that he went on to express the 'hope that the Secretary of State will have no further cause to complain of the frequency of burglarious offences', for which, of course, the Superintendents were alone responsible.

[2] The *London Figaro*, in an obituary notice.

Williamson who survived was a serious man who could easily have become a grim one if he had not been saved by a capacity for friendship. He had always had friends, had always been popular, had always unconsciously depended on being liked. There was never a very close intimacy about his friendships, and perhaps he had always been a trifle formal in the way he talked to the men who meant most to him—a habit which was akin to his hatred of the use of slang. But even if he wasn't very good at expressing deep feelings, he had nevertheless always drawn-in a sense of security through being surrounded by friends.

As he was not given to self-analysis, he would hardly have known on what that sense of security depended: he could not have said that a consciousness of loyalty was at the back of it, even though that was probably the truth. He derived his happiness from regarding his friendships as permanent.

Perhaps his distrust of new things made the old ones more valuable. You could rely on things—such as old friendships—which you had had for a long time and which couldn't change.

Consequently, the discovery that friendship was a shallow thing, and a deceptive thing, and something which didn't count at all against '£25 in gold in a little bag' or a pile of notes in a cigar-box, hit him extremely hard. From the moment when that was forced on him, he became a man who had retired into himself, defensively, a man who was afraid to show his natural gift for friendliness, in case he was tricked again.

'He required knowing,' says Inspector Littlechild, of this period. 'He seemed heavy and unimpressionable.' And Inspector Lansdowne says, 'The trial appeared to shake

Mr. Williamson's faith in his men greatly. He was much less "confiding" after the trial than before.'

Nevertheless, in one way the friendliness peeped out, in spite of all his caution.

The burden of the new department—the Criminal Investigation Department—rested almost entirely on his shoulders. Mr. Howard Vincent could plan and organise—and sometimes had to be restrained. Old John Shore—despite a lamentable lack of education[1]—could be relied on for all the routine work. But it was on Frederick Williamson that there fell the vital task of finding new men—and training them when they were found.

He had always liked young men, he had always enjoyed training them. Once he began to be sure of the men he had chosen, he couldn't help wanting to give them encouragement. Nor could he help being kind. 'I think I might say,' writes Lansdowne, who was one of the first inspectors in the new regime, 'that he was loved by us all, his kindliness of heart being almost proverbial. I have the greatest respect for his memory.' Similarly, Littlechild, who became a Chief-Inspector in 1887, says, 'His faults were few and his virtues were many. His name I shall always revere.'

6

The Criminal Investigation Department had not been in existence for twelve months—and certainly very few of its officers had had any appreciable experience or training—when it was tested over a murder case of great difficulty.

[1] It is said that Shore, whilst writing an official report, once asked a colleague how many times the letter 'r' appeared in the word 'very'. On being told, he said, 'Oh well, I've put two, but I'll put a blot over the second one, and then nobody will notice.'

A coal-cart was being driven along the bank of the Thames near Barnes Bridge, when the driver noticed a wooden box floating downstream, and thought it a good opportunity to secure some flotsam. He brought it ashore, cut the cord around it, and gave the box a kick so that it fell to pieces. Inside it was the nude body of a woman, without a head and with one foot also missing.

The case was at first handled by Inspector Harber of T Division, who was immediately astonished that a woman's body, even without the head, could be crammed into a box that was only one foot two inches high by one foot square. An explanation of that, however, was supplied by the police doctor: he gave it as his opinion that the corpse had been shrunk by being *boiled.*

At that point, Inspector Jones, also of T Divison, took over the case, together with Inspector Dowdell of the Central Office. John Dowdell had been a sergeant only a few months before.

Identification of the headless body seemed impossible, nothing being ascertainable about it except that it was that of a small married woman of about 55. Nobody fulfilling those conditions was on the list of missing persons.

At the end of a week, however, a human foot was found on a dung-heap at Twickenham. It was undoubtedly the missing left foot of the headless corpse—but it did not help very much. Indeed, all the discovery did was to narrow down the district in which the murder must have been committed. A box floating downstream for an unknown time might have travelled a considerable distance; but the fact that the foot was found at Twickenham, coupled with the body having been taken from the water at Barnes, suggested that a circle drawn with a radius of three or four miles from Richmond (which lies midway between Barnes and Twickenham) would be likely to include the scene of the crime.

That being provisionally fixed, the search was intensified in that area. It was argued that as the woman was 'missing' but had not been reported missing, she had presumably lived alone—or with no one except her murderer. She might, for instance, have been a woman 'in small circumstances' who had been killed by her husband, or she might have been a widow alone with one servant. . . .

7

Nothing more happened for twelve days. Then Inspector Pearman, of the police at Richmond, reported that a Mrs. Thomas, 'a small lady of about 54', was missing from that town. There was no exact certainty as to how long she had been missing, but it seemed likely that she had disappeared about eighteen days before—which would have fitted closely with the time when the body was found at Barnes.

There was a Mr. Porter, living at Richmond. Six years before, in the north of England, he had known a girl named Kate Webster, but for that period he had completely lost touch with her. Then—eighteen days ago—she had walked into his house in Richmond and had said that she was not Miss Webster any longer, having married a man named Thomas and been left a widow. Her appearance suggested that she was now fairly well off, so Mr. Porter inferred that her late husband had left her a good deal of money. But when he said something to that effect, she said, No, it wasn't that, her aunt had just died and left her some clothes and jewellery and furniture. She was selling what she didn't want, she said, and did Mr. Porter know anyone who would buy the furniture?

Mr. Porter then introduced a friend of his, a Mr. Church, who heard what there was and said he would take it. Church thereupon hired a van and drove in it, together with Mr. Porter and the Mrs. Thomas, to No. 2, Vine Cottages, Richmond, the home, as Mrs. Thomas explained, of her late aunt.

The men carried out one or two pieces of furniture, and then a woman came out of the next house and said she was Miss Ives, and Mrs. Thomas was her tenant, and what was it all about? Was Mrs. Thomas flitting without the rent paid?

Church and Porter did not know anything about that: indeed, they did not know what to make of it, because they had been told that this was not Mrs. Thomas's house, but Mrs. Thomas's aunt's house—and although, of course, one's aunt could bear the same name as oneself, Mrs. Thomas's aunt was said to be dead, and it was surprising that her landlord, living next door, shouldn't know of that.

Church and Porter therefore went into the house to fetch Mrs. Thomas. She at once became very agitated and said she would go and explain matters to Miss Ives. She would not let the two men stay in the house, and neither would she let them come in with her in to Miss Ives's house, so they stood on the pavement and said to each other, no doubt, that it was 'a rum go'.

After some time, Mrs. Thomas returned, looking very much upset. She announced that she was not going to remove the furniture that day after all—a statement which must have annoyed Mr. Church very much, as he had paid £3 for the hire of the van. In fact, that annoyance must have had something to do with the fact that Church and Porter decided that 'things didn't look right' and that they ought to go and tell the police about it.

That, of course, set Inspector Pearman making enquiries, not so much about Mrs. Thomas's aunt—of whom no one had ever heard—as about the Mrs. Thomas who, it appeared, had lived in the house at Vine Cottages, but had not been seen by the neighbours for more than a fortnight. She was a little woman of between 50 and 60, always very smart and well-dressed: and she had lived alone with one servant, whose name was Kate Webster.

8

By that time, Kate Webster, having taken alarm, no doubt, over the suspicions of Church and Porter—and the knowledge that Miss Ives, when asked, would be certain to disclose her identity—had disappeared. Inspector Dowdell and Inspector Jones went to see Mr. Porter, in the hope of learning something about her past which would tell them where she might have gone. They learnt nothing useful in that way. But Inspector Dowdell had one of those flashes of brilliance with which good detectives solve their cases.

It was a little matter—just a casual question asked of someone who wasn't likely to be able to give any useful answer. But there is a rule in detection—which Superintendent Williamson must certainly have instilled into young Dowdell and all the other men he was training—that successful work requires a large element of luck, and good luck only comes to those who are ready to receive it: while better luck comes to those who actually look for it.

When Mr. Porter was unable to give any useful information, and the two detectives were leaving the house, Dowdell happened to notice a bright-looking boy of fifteen—Mr. Porter's son, Robert. 'Just on the chance', as he himself would have put it, the Inspector asked the boy whether he had seen 'Mrs. Thomas' since the day when she visited his father. . . .

The answer was, 'Oh yes, sir, I saw her the next day, when she asked me to help her carry a box.'

9

It had been a wooden box, about a foot square and tied up with cord, the boy said. And very heavy and awkward, because on one side the handle was missing and it had to be held by the cord. The boy and the woman had carried it between them to Richmond bridge. When they were in the middle of the bridge they stopped and the woman sent the boy on alone, saying that she was meeting a friend there, and giving the box to her.

That was all the boy remembered—at first. But when Inspector Dowdell cross-questioned him, being careful not to put ideas into his mind, he recollected something else: that a moment or two after he left the woman, he heard a splash, as if something had been dropped off the bridge into the river.

10

Thus the chain of events was established. When Mrs. Thomas's house was searched, the missing handle of the wooden box was found, to confirm the boy's story. It was also learnt that neighbours had heard strange sounds coming from the house just after Mrs. Thomas was last seen alive, and that tradesmen—whom Kate Webster had refused to let into the house—had seen the kitchen to be filled with clouds of steam, as if something was being boiled in the copper. . . .

Mrs. Thomas's head was never found. But even without that, there was ample evidence that it was her body which had been crammed, after the process of boiling, into the wooden box, carried to Richmond bridge and thrown into the river, on which it floated downstream for twenty-four hours until it was picked up near Barnes Bridge. And when, a few days later, Inspector Dowdell arrested Kate Webster in a village in Ireland to which she had escaped, there remained little doubt either of her guilt or of her ultimate fate.

PART FIVE

The Third Crisis

CHAPTER 14

Another Threat of Trouble

1

It has already been said that Mr. Howard Vincent studied the methods of the French police before he became Director of Criminal Investigations.

The ways of the French police were quite different from those of the Metropolitan Police. In particular, they had no objection to practices which would have been denounced by the English press as 'the behaviour of spies': and they also saw no objection to the use of *agents provocateurs*.[1] It was unfortunate that Mr. Vincent had a strong leaning towards methods which were quite un-English.

In July 1880, a Mr. Tayler, who was medical assistant at the Provident Dispensary, called at Bow Street police station to denounce a chemist named Thomas Titley—'a young man of respectable appearance'—as an abortioner. He was seen by the Superintendent of E Division, James

[1] The greatest of French detectives, Vidocq, was originally a criminal. After frequent terms of imprisonment and some escapes, he came to realise that he could lead an easier life by betraying old companions to the police. He did this so successfully that he was 'taken on the staff' as an agent: and eventually he became the head of the Paris Sureté.

J. Thomson, who for a short time had been an Inspector at Scotland Yard under Superintendent Williamson. Thomson was keenly interested in the story, but he pointed out that there was no evidence in support of it. Now, if Mr. Tayler could produce something a little more concrete. . . .

The Superintendent then started enquiries and set men to keep watch outside the chemist's shop in Fitzroy Street. Women, he found, frequently came to the side door, after closing time. It was all very suggestive. But still there wasn't evidence. And you could never get women to come forward as witnesses in those cases.

After three months, Mr. Tayler came again, this time with a young man who had been Titley's assistant in the shop and had been dismissed. The ex-assistant had a hair-raising story to tell, but it mainly consisted of 'I thought he was doing—', 'I came to the conclusion that he must be doing—' and so on. It would have been of no value in a court of law.

Nevertheless, when he came to put all that he had heard together, Superintendent Thomson had not the slightest doubt of Titley's guilt.

He therefore put the matter in front of Superintendent Williamson: and Williamson took him to Mr. Howard Vincent.

2

Reading between the lines—and knowing what we do on the point of personal character—we may assume that Chief-Superintendent Williamson was profoundly shocked at the plan for dealing with the case which the Director of Criminal Investigations put forward. He would have protested with vigour, and Vincent—good-humouredly

—would have laughed at his scruples. Nobody at the Sureté would have hesitated for a moment over employing such a trick.

There would be no evidence of value unless it could be shown that Titley had actually performed an illegal operation—or had contrived the same effect by the use of drugs. No woman who had been dealt with in that way would come forward. And it was not permissible to send a pregnant woman specially to ask for that kind of help, because that would come under the heading of inciting Titley to commit a crime.

But supposing the man could be induced to supply drugs on the strength of a false story, when in fact there was no pregnant woman to whom they were to be given. . . .

3

Inspector O'Callaghan of the Divisional Police was then put in charge of the case. He appears to have entered into the spirit of the thing, without in the least sharing Williamson's scruples. First, he took into his confidence his assistant, Sergeant Shrives. He then got hold of a Mrs. Martha Diffey, a female searcher at Bow Street and the wife of a pensioned police-constable. Mrs. Diffey had no scruples either: she did what she was told to do—and did it very well.

She went one night to the side door of Titley's shop and said she wanted to speak to him privately. He let her in, and she told him that she was the mother of nine children[1] and what she wanted to speak about was 'a little affair about her daughter who was in the family way'. She said

[1] Actually, she had two daughters only. This embellishment seems to suggest that she was enjoying herself.

'the person responsible' was the master of the house where her daughter worked as a domestic servant.

Mr. Titley was sympathetic. He made no pretence of not understanding why Mrs. Diffey had come to him or what he was being asked to do: on the contrary, he explained that 'his business' generally lay with ladies who had got into trouble while their husbands were abroad. But he said that while he quite understood the difficulties he had to be extremely cautious, and therefore he must see the girl herself before he consented to 'prescribe' for her.

Mrs. Diffey said that was natural, of course, but her daughter wouldn't come, being shy . . . Mr. Titley said he was very sorry, but in that case he couldn't do anything.

When Inspector O'Callaghan heard that, he reported to Mr. Vincent. Was he, he wanted to know, now to get hold of a girl?

That, of course, couldn't be allowed for a minute. The essential thing, in order to avoid an accusation of 'inciting' was that there must be no girl in the case. But there was already the mother of the non-existent girl, and now—Vincent said—there could be the non-existent girl's seducer. Or at any rate a letter from him. Inspector O'Callaghan could sit down and write it.

Mr. Howard Vincent never wrote a work of fiction, but that letter which he dictated to O'Callaghan suggests that he could have done. It was extremely realistic and plausible, admitting that the girl was 'employed in our house' and stating that the situation now on hand was a very difficult one. Later, if matters were allowed to develop, the writer would be put to expense, and in the circumstances he would rather incur the expense now and

Picture Post Library

HOWARD VINCENT

"He had his own way of doing things"

save the development. So if Mr. Titley could see his way——

When the letter was written, there was the question of a signature for it. And there Vincent's sense of humour peeped out again. 'Oh, we'll call this man "Williamson",' he said.

4

Actually, the letter was signed only with the initials, H. W. (presumably because it was realised that no man would put his name to a letter of that kind) and the name 'Henry Williamson' was held in reserve. As will be seen, it was used later.

Mrs. Diffey took the letter to Titley. He was impressed by it, but he said that what he was being asked to do would mean a heavy prison sentence for him if he was found out, and he must take every precaution. If he couldn't see the girl, he must at least see the man, the writer of that letter.

Again O'Callaghan went to Vincent, who of course saw no difficulty in that development. 'Henry Williamson' could easily be produced: the Inspector must have a man who would look well in that part.

The Inspector had, of course: and accordingly, the following evening, Detective-Sergeant Stroud, of E Division of the Metropolitan Police, was suitably attired in a frock coat and tall hat, and presented himself, with Mrs. Diffey, at Titley's shop. His name, he told Titley, was Henry Williamson.

He said very much what had been said in the letter, and flourished a pocket-book containing five £5 notes.

Finally, Mr. Titley agreed to do what was necessary, and produced two bottles of medicine. Sergeant Stroud then tendered one of the £5 notes in payment—and was very much surprised when he received £4 16s. as change.

The next day, after the contents of the bottles had been analysed, Inspector O'Callaghan, with Sergeant Shrives and Sergeant Stroud, went to the shop and put Titley under arrest. The young chemist said, on being charged, that he had only been trying to help some people in distress—a statement which may well have had a considerable grain of truth in it, seeing that he had only charged 4/- when he was offered £5.

Both in the police court and at the Old Bailey, Titley was ably defended: the police witnesses were drastically cross-examined, and the fact that the prisoner had been tricked was made extremely clear. It was established that the trickery had not been a mere piece of smartness on the part of any underling, but had been at least countenanced by the Superintendent of E Division and by the Director of Criminal Investigations.[1] Defending Counsel had much to say on that.

Nevertheless, Titley was found guilty by the jury and was sentenced to eighteen months hard labour. In passing sentence, the judge had his own remarks to make.

'One important part of the question,' he said, 'is as to the means adopted for entrapping the prisoner into a crime. I regret that that course was taken. It is a matter of extreme difficulty as to how far deception in such cases is justifiable. But here, there is a fluency and readiness of invention, and a facility of employing *spies* to go and lie, which is very painful to witness. In particular, there is

[1] It is remarkable that, even when faced with the hint given by the name 'Williamson', no one drew attention to the fact that no part of the responsibility was assigned to the Chief-Superintendent of the Criminal Investigation Department.

that letter which purported to be a letter written by a young man who had misbehaved himself in relation to a young girl. There is no such young man, and there was no such young girl, and, in fact, the letter was written, as we have been told from the witness-box, by Inspector O'Callaghan, for the express purpose of deceiving the prisoner. I am quite satisfied that the prisoner did not need very much inducement to do something illegal for his own profit, but at the same time I own that I think anyone who had had any regard for his own integrity—whether a policeman or anyone else—would have refused to write that letter.'

The press naturally took the matter up—*The Times*, for instance, devoted three columns to a report of the case.

It may be thought that Mr. Howard Vincent was not particularly disturbed about that: he had his own ways of doing things, and didn't mind what the newspapers said. But he felt rather differently about it when he received a telephone message[1] to the effect that a Bill of Indictment had been preferred against Inspector O'Callaghan, Sergeant Shrives, Sergeant Stroud and Mrs. Diffey for conspiring to incite Titley to commit a crime.

Mr. Vincent was prepared to fight the case on the ground that 'the action taken was in the public interest and in the execution of public duty': but (fortunately or unfortunately, since that defence would have raised points of exceptional interest) the hastily-drawn indictment was found to be 'bad law' and the case could not proceed.

'I never was so pleased,' wrote Howard Vincent afterwards, 'as when those excellent officers stepped out of the dock . . . *They* were in no way whatever to blame.'

[1] This new invention had just been installed at Scotland Yard.

5

That, however, was not the end of the matter. The newspapers had more to say, and questions were asked in the House of Commons about the conduct of the police and whether the officers responsible should not be prosecuted by the Crown.

Thus, once again, and only four years after the last major crisis, Scotland Yard was in disgrace. This time, however, the matter was not allowed to go into extremes. There was now no question of dishonest action by the police and therefore a prosecution would have given quite a wrong idea to the public.

In reply to the questions, the Home Secretary announced that he had given directions that 'no such method shall be resorted to for the future without direct communication or authority from the Home Office.' But at the same time he told the House that 'The other day the police had information that another man had been carrying on practices similar to those of Titley, but they had insufficient evidence to prosecute. Subsequently, both the woman and the child died, and a prosecution will now follow; but this is a prosecution which will have cost two lives.'

He also said that although practices of trickery in such cases would not in future be resorted to without Home Office authority, the giving of that authority was a responsibility from which the Secretary of State ought not to shrink. In announcing that there would be no prosecution of Inspector O'Callaghan and the others, he said, 'There is a danger that the confidence of the public may be shaken in the good faith of the police; and, of all the evils that could occur, that would be the greatest.'

Thus this, the third crisis faced by Scotland Yard in twenty-one years, was not allowed to shake it to its foundations. It had become an institution which was essential to the life of the British people, and it had to continue with public approval and confidence. The Metropolitan Police are no longer spoken of as 'Peel's bloody gang.'

PART SIX

Sequel to The Third Crisis

CHAPTER 15

The Persistent Sergeant

1

Whether merely as a coincidence or not, it was from that date that Howard Vincent began to find an outlet for his excess energies in reforming and modernizing the *Police Gazette*, and in writing a *Police Code and Manual of the Criminal Law*. When a new series of Fenian outrages started, he became very active in hunting Irishmen, but his biography, which before the Titley case had dealt with his 'unconventional methods' of dealing with crime, afterwards only mentions one ordinary crime in which he took a personal interest. And within three and a half years he had tired of his work as Director of Criminal Investigations, and had resigned on the ground that it 'offered no prospect of advancement'. But, of course, it does not necessarily follow that all that would not have happened if his 'unconventional methods' had been welcomed with general approbation and had not had to be publicly 'excused' by the Home Secretary.

2

The Irish troubles were very serious, and although the Irish Branch was then in existence to deal with them the Criminal Investigation Department had also to play its part, and once again its senior officers, including Chief-Superintendent Williamson, had to make frequent journeys to Liverpool, to Manchester and to Dublin.

In fact, the men of the Central office were very much taken off their proper job at that time, and consequently the usual practice of associating Scotland Yard men with the divisional detectives on important crimes could very often not be followed, because Great Scotland Yard had no men available.

That, however, mattered very much less than it would have done a few years earlier—because to a considerable extent the Scotland Yard Inspectors were recently promoted and barely trained, whereas some of the divisional inspectors were of long standing and highly competent.

Thus the divisional men now proved that the old system of 'supervision' was entirely unnecessary.

3

Late in the evening, on December 1st, 1882, two women were going home through the streets of Dalston when they saw a police constable struggling with a man whom they assumed to be 'a drunk'. Then they heard four shots, and the constable fell to the ground and the man ran away. Without stopping to see how badly the constable was hurt, the two women ran to give the alarm at the police station.

The constable was George Cole, a young married man who had only been in the Force for ten months. He had been shot through the head, and was speechless until his death a few hours later, so the story of what had happened had to be pieced together from what there was in the way of evidence.

The constable's beat would have taken him past a Baptist chapel, a few minutes before he was shot. In the grounds of the chapel were found two chisels and a wooden wedge of the kind which housebreakers use. Taking the two incidents of the night to be connected, it was assumed that a man had prepared to break into the chapel—where, among other articles of value, there was the sacramental plate—and had been caught in the act and arrested by Constable Cole. Then, when he was being taken to the police station, the man had tried to break away, there had been the struggle which the two women had seen, and finally the murder.

It had happened on a dark and foggy night, and, if that had been all, there would have been little chance of the man being identified and found. But a short time before a Sergeant Cobb, together with a constable, had passed the chapel and had noticed a young man 'hanging about'.

There were, of course, other reasons beside crime why a young man might hang about in the streets at night, and there would therefore have been no reason to connect this one with criminal intentions—except that he seemed furtive and not at all anxious to meet policemen. Moreover, Sergeant Cobb knew him by sight: he was a lad of nineteen, named Thomas Henry Orrock, who lived in the neighbourhood and attended services at that Baptist chapel—although, according to Sergeant Cobb, religious instruction hadn't done him much good so far. He had not actually been in the hands of the police, but that, again according to Sergeant Cobb, was only because he wasn't old enough to be as bad as he was going to be, later on.

In any case, the sergeant was suspicious at the sight of him, and remarked to the constable that young Orrock was 'up to something'. But there was nothing he could be charged with except 'loitering with intent', and that was no good when there was no evidence of the 'intent'.

Sergeant Cobb therefore walked on, making a mental note that if there was any crime in the neighbourhood that night he would give some attention to young Orrock.

4

A few hours later, the sergeant wanted very badly to 'give some attention' to Orrock: but doing that would not make any difference to poor Constable Cole, who was lying stiff in the mortuary.

Sergeant Cobb was a kindly man, and he had liked George Cole. Now, it seemed to him that Cole would have been alive if young Orrock had at least been kept under observation. Inspector Glass, of N. Division, who took charge of the case, pointed out that there wasn't the slightest evidence that Orrock was connected with it: but Cobb was in a state of certainty and self-reproach which did not need evidence.

He regarded himself as personally responsible for George Cole's death.

Orrock was found and brought to the Dalston police station, but when he was put on an identity parade neither of the two women who had witnessed the murder was able to pick him out. There was therefore nothing for it but to let him go—at any rate until some evidence could be found.

The only evidence at that time—if, indeed, it was evidence—lay in the fact that one of the two chisels found near the window of the Baptist chapel had scratched on it some lettering. It wasn't very clear, but it might possibly be read as 'rock', which could be part of the name 'Orrock'. But on the other hand, it might be nothing of the sort. You just couldn't tell, and it was no use charging a man and taking him to Court on evidence as vague as that.

Apart from which, Orrock could not now be taken to Court on any evidence, even if there had been some, because, immediately after the identity parade, he had completely disappeared.

Even that fact was not necessarily suspicious. Young men of bad character often disappeared in Dalston—particularly after they had been dragged to the police station and put on identity parades. It just seemed to them a reasonable precaution, when the police were 'getting nasty'.

There was therefore no proper reason why Orrock should be suspected of the murder, and Inspector Glass did not trouble about him any more. But Sergeant Cobb still had his self-reproaches: he could not bring George Cole back to life, but he meant to avenge him by getting Thomas Henry Orrock hanged for murdering him.

5

The Fenian troubles continued, occupying more and more of the attention of the authorities at Scotland Yard.

They certainly could not have spared anyone to help in a murder case at Dalston even if it had been worth while; and, just to look for an unknown man who had disappeared into the fog on a dark night without leaving any traces or clues, it was *not* worth while. Despite a natural desire on the part of the police that a constable's murder, particularly, should be followed by a hanging, it was obvious that that crime would have to go onto the list of unsolvable cases.

On March 15th, 1883, a dynamite bomb was exploded in the office of the *Times* newspaper, and in the evening of the same day another went off in a government office in Whitehall. It was a time of great public outcry, of newspaper agitation, of rumours, alarums and excursions. No one knew where the next bomb would explode. . . .

In October, one exploded near Charing Cross, another by Paddington Station, and a third on the Underground Railway. Sixty people were injured.

Early in 1884, a time-bomb was hidden in a portmanteau which two Irishmen deposited in the cloak-room at Victoria, and part of the station was blown up. That meant still more work for the Scotland Yard detectives, as men had to be stationed in every cloak-room to search for bombs in every package or portmanteau that was left there—and that was not all fruitless work, for bombs were actually discovered, just in time, at Charing Cross, Ludgate Hill and Paddington.

The small staff of the Central Office at Scotland Yard were continually rushed here and there, in answer to rumours[1] and to deal with threats.

[1] There was even one rumour that dismounted Irishmen were practising cavalry tactics in the 'back kitchen' of a restaurant run by an Irishman named Jerry Flannigan, in Theobald's Road.

Consequently, ordinary work was neglected and the criminals had an easy time—except for what the divisional detectives and the ordinary police could do against them.

6

Meanwhile, Sergeant Cobb of the Dalston Police had never forgotten about Thomas Henry Orrock.

For more than a year, while doing his other duties, he had been continually hoping to hear something about the man—or about Constable Cole's murder. At last, he met a man named Mortimer—not a man who would have talked at all to a police sergeant if he had thought he was doing any harm to his pals, but one who didn't mind talking about little things that had nothing to do with any crime. So one day Mortimer told Sergeant Cobb that about a year before he had been with three men named Miles, Evans and Orrock to do a little target practice with a revolver, against a tree on Tottenham Marshes.

There was nothing in that, of course—except that it had to do with Orrock and a revolver.

Without displaying too much interest in the story, Sergeant Cobb managed to persuade Mortimer to come with him to the Marshes. Then he referred to the story: 'Shooting at a tree, weren't you? Any idea which tree it was?'

Mortimer showed him the tree.

Sergeant Cobb, of course, did not seem to mind about the tree, after all. But after a while, he sent Mortimer home while he himself stayed on. . . . And when he was alone he got to work on the tree with his knife, digging out bullets.

One of them was of the same calibre as the bullet which a doctor, a year before, had taken out of Constable Cole's brain.

7

The next step was to trace the two men, Miles and Evans, who had been with Mortimer and Orrock on Tottenham Marshes that day. Sergeant Cobb found them, but they did not want to talk. So he told them—quite untruthfully—that he was after them both for Constable Cole's murder. Then they were in a hurry to tell everything they knew.

Orrock, it appeared, had bought the revolver, from an advertisement in the *Bazaar, Exchange and Mart*, for 10*s.* 6*d.*

On the night of the crime, Orrock had been with Miles and Evans and had put up a plan for breaking into the Baptist chapel and stealing the sacramental plate. He was quite prepared to do the job himself, but he wanted help in carrying away the loot. Miles and Evans—at any rate according to their own story—had not wanted to have anything to do with it; but they hadn't minded staying in Orrock's company, in various public houses, till dark, and they had even gone out with him to buy a bull's-eye lantern which he needed for the robbery.

When night came on and the fog settled down, Orrock suggested that they should start. That time, at any rate, Miles and Evans did say 'No'—there was evidence that they were both in a public house till long after the murder had been committed. So Orrock set out for the Baptist chapel alone. He had with him housebreaking implements, the bull's-eye lantern—and his revolver.

8

Thus it was established that Thomas Henry Orrock had set out to commit a crime that night, and that if he had held to his original plan he would have been near Constable Cole's beat at the time of the murder. It was thus a fair presumption that he was the murderer. The question was whether the circumstantial evidence was strong enough. Supposing he put up the defence that he had changed his mind and not gone near the chapel, so that anyone arrested there by Constable Cole must have been someone else?

The divisional police therefore started extensive enquiries among the people in London who undertake the sharpening of tools such as chisels. At last they found a woman who said that when such tools were left with her, she always scratched the name of the owner on the metal: and she identified the scratched lettering, 'r–o–c–k', as a part of the name 'Orrock'. There was thus final evidence that Orrock had been at the scene of the crime when the murder was committed.

Only there was no sign of the man, who had disappeared completely from mortal sight, more than twelve months before. Sergeant Cobb had at last got his proofs of Orrock's guilt. What he hadn't got, still, was the man himself, to be sent to the gallows.

He went on searching for him.

9

Sixteen cakes of dynamite, with a fuse, were discovered, just in time, at the foot of the Nelson column. A bomb exploded in Gower Street. An attempt was made to blow up London Bridge. A bomb was placed in Westminster Hall, and only discovered a few minutes before it was due to explode. And the offices in Old Scotland Yard which were used by the Irish Branch of the Metropolitan Police were blown to pieces—although fortunately the last man had gone out of them a quarter of an hour before.

The Fenians were thus becoming more and more active. The counter-measures of the police were also becoming more and more active. But although several Irishmen were arrested and charged—and some were sentenced to penal servitude for life—there were always others to take their places. It wasn't like ordinary crime: you were fighting an organisation, and not a number of individuals. In a sense, of course, that was exactly like crime, for you could never end crime, however many criminals you sent to prison or even hanged. But dealing with criminals was a much more satisfactory task than dealing with mad Irishmen. For one thing, criminals rarely did anything that was strikingly original. . . .

10

Sergeant Cobb was still searching for Orrock. He could not think how it was possible for a man to disappear so completely, when the police all over the country had been warned to look for him. Then the idea suddenly came: there was, of course, one way by which a man like Orrock could hide in almost perfect safety. . . .

Thus, in due course, and after a search that altogether had lasted the better part of two years, Thomas Henry Orrock was found by Sergeant Cobb—in Coldbath-fields Prison.

Or not, at first, found, exactly. There was a man there,

it was reported, who had been serving a sentence for a minor felony, for nearly two years. His description resembled that of Orrock. But he had not been sentenced under that name and, when challenged, he denied emphatically that it was his name. Moreover, when he was put on an identity parade with six other convicts, Sergeant Cobb, who had come very eagerly to Coldbath-fields on receipt of the news, was quite unable to recognise him.

So the seven men on the parade were dismissed and ordered to file out. As they walked past Sergeant Cobb—perhaps it was through a trick of the light—he immediately knew one of them for Orrock: he had not recognised the man full-face, and had said so, but, side-view, he saw the face which had remained photographed in his memory ever since he had seen it, from the same angle, under a street-lamp in the fog, two years before in Dalston.

In December, 1885, Orrock was hanged: he left behind him a confession. At the trial, the judge recorded the jury's strong approval of the persistence of Sergeant Cobb.[1]

11

The dynamite outrages became so serious that the Government was forced to adopt new methods of dealing with the Fenians. It was certainly not enough for the Metropolitan Police to rush from the scene of one explosion to that of the next: nor did it help appreciably when judges spoke with dreadful sternness of the enormity of the outrages, as they sentenced captured and convicted Irishmen to long terms of imprisonment. The men who were captured were mostly underlings, anyway, and it was becoming obvious that the 'campaign' would only

[1] In spite of this, Sergeant Cobb never reached the rank of Inspector.

end when either the leaders were captured, or advance news could be obtained of their plans, so that their attacks could be forestalled.

This was, to a large extent, an 'underground' war, and the only way to meet it was by underground tactics. Therefore attempts were made, by British agents sent to America, to win over some of the Irish leaders there. They went on the attempt with full purses.

12

By that time, Mr. Howard Vincent had resigned and entered Parliament. The title of 'Director of Criminal Investigations' was then abolished, and his successor, Mr. James Monro, who had been Inspector-General of Police in Bengal, appeared as Assistant Commissioner, Crime Department. The change of title made no difference in the function and work, except that it brought the C.I.D. more definitely under the orders of the Commissioner of the Metropolitan Police and thus put a curb on 'unconventional methods'.

Mr. Monro only stayed for four years in that post, although later he was appointed Commissioner of the Metropolitan Police.

Early in 1887, he had to deal with a case which arose out of the new 'underground' methods of the Government against the Fenians. A minor Irish-American leader, who for some years had been receiving money from British agents, travelled from the United States and got as far as Boulogne on his way to London. His mission, for which he was coming to England, was no less than to arrange for the explosion of a bomb in Westminster Abbey during the Queen's Jubilee celebrations.

From Boulogne, however, he wrote to Scotland Yard, offering to betray the whole plan, together with the names of his confederates—in return for a considerable sum in gold.

It would have been fully in accordance with Government policy at the time to have paid the money and then to have arrested all the conspirators in England, while the bribed leader returned to America with a fortune. But it so happened that there were a number of men at the head of police affairs, just then, whose views of public conduct, though by no means the same, united in condemning that policy.

There was Munro, who thought it 'discreditable' that public funds should be used for lining the pockets of a would-be assassin: there was Chief-Superintendent Williamson, an upright man who had acquired a horror of bribery—he wouldn't have thought it made much moral difference whether you received the bribes or gave them: and there was Dr. Robert Anderson (at that time engaged in Secret Service work and a year later to succeed Mr. Monro as Assistant Commissioner) who had the strongest of religious and moral principles.

Consequently, a better scheme was sought. Obviously, the life of the Queen had to be saved at all costs—the conspirators working for this outrage had all to be rounded up. But couldn't that be done without rewarding a man who, by his own confession, would do the crime if he wasn't paid well for selling his friends?

It all depended on getting the man in Boulogne to talk—without his knowing that what he said would be reported to Scotland Yard. Eventually, a scheme was devised; but then the difficulty was to find someone who could carry it out. Ten years or more earlier, the man for the work would unquestionably have been Chief-Inspector Nathaniel Druscovich: he would have done it well, and with enjoyment. But now— Chief-Inspector Greenham was fluent in Italian, but that was of no value in Boulogne. Inspector von Tornow[1] spoke German, but that was no good either. Chief-Superintendent Williamson spoke French, certainly, but he had never had time to travel much, and he did not know Boulogne: besides, he was now a sick man, worn out by long hours of hard work during the troublesome years.

But there was one man who had all the necessary qualifications, and could be trusted in every way: Superintendent Williamson's old friend, James J. Thomson. He had recently retired on a well-earned pension, after eighteen years' service as Superintendent of E Division of the Metropolitan Police. He was a linguist, he knew Boulogne 'like the back of his hand', and he had once had a detective's training.

13

Accordingly, a Mr. Thomson went with his wife for a holiday in Boulogne. They put up at a certain hotel, and of course it was only natural for Mrs. Thomson to get into conversation with an American lady who was also staying there. It was equally natural for the two wives to introduce their husbands after dinner, and for a very pleasant evening to be spent. In the course of that first pleasant evening it came out that the Americans were held up in Boulogne, awaiting an important business letter which was expected from London, and that they were finding

[1] Von Tornow had been forgiven for 'desertion' at the time when the chief-inspectors were on trial, and had been re-instated and promoted.

the time hang heavily on their hands, their situation being somewhat worse than it would otherwise have been because neither of them spoke the French language.

Mr. Thomson, it then appeared, was quite an experienced Continental traveller, a good linguist, and a man who knew Boulogne very well and had the entrée to all the possibilities of amusement that the town afforded. And of course if he could help his new American friend in any way— Why shouldn't they make up a party of four, and go and enjoy themselves for the evening?

Thus the friendship quickly ripened. It progressed still more after Mr. Thomson had confessed to Irish forbears, to pro-Irish sentiments, and to views concerning the British Crown and Government which were very nearly those of an anarchist.

The American had the same sentiments entirely.

Also he developed a fondness for French wines, of which Mr. Thomson had copious knowledge.

And so, before many days had passed, the Irish-American was talking very freely and candidly to his new friend.

14

It was only when all had been told that Mr. Thomson went to the Post Office and despatched a long telegram to Chief-Superintendent Williamson.

A few days later, another Englishman arrived at the hotel. He spoke French very well, but nevertheless he appeared to be one of those travellers who like the sound of their own language when abroad, and so it came about that a fifth place was laid at the table of the Thomsons and their American friends. The newcomer said his name was Frederick Williamson. When the wine was circulating, a little later, he explained casually that he was a superintendent of police at Scotland Yard. . . .

The American was momentarily taken aback: then he became very anxious to know whether Mr. Superintendent Williamson was there on business or purely for pleasure. Mrs. Thomson, on the other hand, was not taken aback at all: she said, rather gushingly, that being a detective must be perfectly fascinating, and it had always been the dream of her life to know a policeman.

Still, Mrs. Thomson managed to tear herself away from the party before very long, as also did Mr. Thomson. Superintendent Williamson then had a very straight talk with the American, telling him—much to his surprise—that the information he had offered to sell was not required, and warning him that he would be arrested immediately if he ever set foot in England.

There was a large number of arrests of Irishmen in England during the next few weeks. No bomb was exploded in Westminster Abbey during the celebration of Queen Victoria's jubilee.

PART SEVEN

The Fourth Crisis

CHAPTER 16

The Yard Against Itself

1

By August, 1888, there had been several further changes at Scotland Yard.

Chief-Superintendent Williamson was a sick man, with heart trouble, and it was realised that he would not be able to continue at work very much longer. But he had had far more experience than anyone else, and his advice was very valuable: so a sinecure post was found for him, where he would not have to be active, and yet would be available for counsel when that was needed. Thus Williamson became the first Chief Constable of the Criminal Investigation Department.[1]

Chief-Inspector John Shore succeeded him as Superintendent: there were five Chief-Inspectors (Greenham, Neame, Butcher, Littlechild and Swanson) and fourteen inspectors. Six of the inspectors had only just been promoted, but the other eight were old hands.

Thus, as far as the regular personnel of the Department was concerned, the position was entirely sound.

[1] An appointment which is not regularly filled.

Among the higher officials, however, affairs were not nearly so happy.

Colonel Henderson had gone from the office of Commissioner of the Metropolitan Police, and had been succeeded by Sir Charles Warren, an autocratic, elderly soldier who wanted to run everything in his own way—the military way. He was inclined, moreover, to regard his fellow men (or at any rate the civilians amongst them) as fools, and not to suffer them gladly. One of the 'fools', in his opinion, was the Home Secretary, who was above him; another was Mr. James Monro, who, as Assistant Commissioner (Crime Department) in charge of the C.I.D., was immediately under him.

The Home Secretary presumably regarded the Commissioner as a valuable man, even if a cantankerous one: and for a time nothing very much happened in that direction.

Mr. Monro, however, held very much the same opinion of Sir Charles Warren as Sir Charles Warren held of Mr. Monro. Consequently, there were 'bickerings', with plenty of faults on both sides. Neither man, it would seem, was at all tactful towards the other. 'Every morning for the last few weeks there has been a protracted conference between Mr. Monro and the principal detective inspectors, and the information furnished to the Commissioner in regard to these conferences has been, the Commissioner states, of the scantiest character.'[1]

The fact was that Mr. Monro wanted to run his own Department, and Sir Charles Warren wanted to run all Departments, including Mr. Monro's. It was impossible for that situation to continue: and while it continued the

[1] *The Times.*

efficiency of the Criminal Investigation Department was considerably lessened.

2

On August 7th, a prostitute named Martha Turner was murdered in a street in Whitechapel. That, of course, was not an event of much moment from the point of view of the authorities at Scotland Yard: it was merely one of the numerous cases reported in the daily list. The divisional detectives were left to deal with it. The authorities continued to bicker amongst themselves.

3

A fortnight later, Mr. Monro resigned his post as Assistant Commissioner, and Dr. Robert Anderson was appointed to succeed him.

Dr. Anderson had been in the Prison Department, and had done secret service work in connection with the Irish troubles. One of his major activities was the writing of a very large number of books on religious matters: he had very firm opinions, particularly on religion and morals, and was never afraid of expressing them. But he was not a quarrelsome man—nor one given to 'bickering'. 'During all my official life,' he wrote later in his autobiography, 'I have never failed to "get on" with any man, no matter what his moods, if only he was honourable and straight . . . My relations with Sir Charles Warren were always easy and pleasant.'

Nevertheless, he had certain characteristics—and held certain opinions—which did not entirely fit him for some of the work he had to do.

4

During the night before Dr. Anderson took up his post at Scotland Yard, a prostitute named Mary Ann Nichols was murdered in a street in Whitechapel. That, of course, was not of much moment—but it was disturbing that there should be another woman of the 'unfortunate' class murdered in the same district, only twenty-four days after the previous crime. Still, such things happened. No doubt the divisional detectives would be able to find the murderer, though it would be well for them to have some assistance from the Central Office, particularly as the newspapers were inclined to give some prominence to the two murders.

About twelve months before, Inspector F. G. Abberline had been brought onto the Scotland Yard staff from H. Division, which worked in Whitechapel and the Commercial Road. Inspector Abberline was an officer of considerable experience and skill,[1] and he had a thorough knowledge both of East End topography and of the people of that district. There could, therefore, be no more appropriate officer to be put in charge of murder cases in Whitechapel.

There was, of course, no need to do more than that—particularly in view of the class of women who had been murdered. That, at any rate, was Dr. Anderson's view.

Dr. Anderson had, moreover, only accepted his post on the condition that he had a month's holiday (in accordance with his doctor's advice) before he properly took up the work. He therefore spent one week at Scotland

[1] He was one of the 14 Inspectors 'appointed' to Divisions, without being put on probation, when the C.I.D. was first formed.

Yard in finding out what he would have to do there, when he returned from the holiday.

On the night of September 8th, a prostitute named Annie Chapman was murdered in a street in Whitechapel. As had happened in the other murders, the body was horribly ripped and mutilated.

On the morning of September 9th, Dr. Anderson, the new Assistant Commissioner (Crime Department) in charge of the C.I.D., started for Switzerland, on his holiday.

5

That third in the series of murders committed by 'Jack the Ripper' brought public excitement to a high pitch. It seemed as if the most devilish murderer of all time was at large in London. No one knew when he would strike next—but everyone was sure he would strike again. No one knew *whom* he would strike next: the fact that he had only attacked women 'of a certain class' was ignored in something very closely resembling a public panic, and even respectable women in the West End of London were afraid to go out at night.

The newspapers devoted many columns to the murders. A 'Vigilance Committee' was set up in the East End. Parties of men from other parts of London went down to Whitechapel every night to help patrol the streets—some men even dressed themselves as women in the hope that they would be attacked and so would have a chance of collaring the assassin.

The Police were extremely active. Sir Charles Warren regarded it as being as much a case for the Metropolitan Police as for the Criminal Investigation Department, since, as there were no reliable clues of any sort to the identity of the murderer, the best chance seemed to be to catch him red-handed when he tried to strike again. That could only be done by increasing the patrols in the Whitechapel streets—so, 'Sir Charles Warren has sent every available man into the East End.'[1]

Meanwhile, the C.I.D. followed up everything that showed the slightest sign of leading towards a clue. . . .

6

Yet the situation of the Criminal Investigation Department in this case was very peculiar.

Chief Constable Williamson, who knew more about detective work than anyone else—and who should therefore have been permanently at the scene of the crimes, directing operations if not personally conducting them—was a very sick man and unable to do more than sit at his desk in Scotland Yard. Superintendent Shore, with the whole weight of the Department on his shoulders, was far too busy to leave his office, even for such an important case as this: there were other major crimes to demand his attention, including one unsolvable one concerned with the body of a woman, headless and without limbs, and wrapped in a piece of black petticoat, which was found in the basement of the partly-constructed building which was to be the headquarters of the Metropolitan Police and the C.I.D., with the name of New Scotland Yard.

And after four years under an Assistant Commissioner who had spent much of his time in bickerings with the Commissioner, the Department was now under a very new Chief—who was on holiday in Switzerland.

[1] *The Times.*

Consequently, the case was handled very much by routine, without any exceptional measures as far as the C.I.D. was concerned. A large force of divisional detectives dealt with it, with one Inspector from Scotland Yard to assist them. . . . 'Since September 30th, Inspectors Reid, Moore, and Nairn, with Sergeants Thicke, Godley, McCarthy and Pearce' (all of H. Division) 'have been constantly engaged under the direction of Inspector Abberline. Each officer has had on the average, during the last six weeks, to make some thirty enquiries weekly in different parts of the metropolis and the suburbs. No fewer than 1,400 letters have been received by the police.'[1]

7

The newspapers were extremely critical of the way the enquiries were being conducted. As each fresh murder was announced, every morning paper and every evening paper devoted a whole page or more of its space to the account of it, with street plans, interviews with anyone who had seen anything, and speculations on who the murderer could be. More pages were filled on the following days. And every paper published a leading article on these 'atrocious crimes'.

Each of those leading articles blamed someone, either directly or by innuendo. Even those which carefully explained that the police could not be expected to solve a case which contained no clues went out of their way to say 'It does not at all follow that the police are useless or corrupt.'

The Home Secretary was assailed, partly because he was the Home Secretary, but more particularly because

[1] *The Times.*

he had refused to offer a reward for 'information'[1] and would not go further than to promise a pardon to any accomplice who would betray the actual murderer. *The Daily Telegraph* expressed its opinions quite plainly: 'London this morning will talk and think of nothing else except these new proofs of the continued presence in our streets of some monster or monsters in human form . . . And where, forsooth, is Mr. Matthews all this while? . . . Is the Home Office waiting for Nos. 7, 8 and 9 in this ghastly catalogue of slayings? . . . Justice—personified unhappily just now in the helpless, heedless, useless figure of the Rt. Hon. Henry Matthews—ought at length to arouse herself . . . in order to unearth this unspeakable villain whose deeds appal a whole kingdom.'

Sir Charles Warren—'this hopeless and conspicious failure'[2]—was assailed, partly because he was a soldier playing the part of a policeman, but more particularly because he had the Army man's dislike of co-operating with the Press; and also because of an unfortunate affair connected with bloodhounds.

The idea of using bloodhounds to track the murderer appealed very much to the public imagination, and the idea was taken up by the Press. It also appealed to Sir Charles Warren, and he was publicly seen exercising bloodhounds in Hyde Park. Then the day came when 'Inspector Abberline sent a message to the Commissioner, asking for the bloodhounds.' But no bloodhounds appeared on the scene of the crime, then or ever . . . The explanation of that appeared later in the columns of *The Morning*

[1] This system had only recently been abandoned, as unwise and dangerous, and could hardly be immediately re-started. Besides, it seemed obvious that no one had any true information to give, so that the offer of a reward would only have wasted the time of the police in dealing with useless correspondence.

[2] *The Pall Mall Gazette.*

SIR CHARLES WARREN TRYING OUT THE BLOODHOUNDS IN HYDE PARK

from a set of drawings by ***Louis Wain***

Post: 'The non-appearance of the bloodhounds yesterday is accounted for by the fact that during recent trials in Surrey the animals bolted, and have not been recovered.' The Press had a lot to say about Sir Charles Warren and his bloodhounds.

Individual members of the Police were not attacked. But the Force as a whole certainly did not escape. For example, *The Daily News* said in one of its leading articles:

> 'It is impossible to avoid the depressing conviction that the Police are about to fail once more . . . The Police have done nothing, they have thought of nothing . . . The most astonishing of the East End mysteries is the mystery of the utter paralysis of energy and intelligence on the part of the Police.'

8

Dr. Anderson knew all about what was happening. In his autobiography, he tells us that he read the English newspapers and found that they were commenting on his absence from his post at such a time. He also received official letters and reports from Whitehall. And after three weeks, he says, he decided to spend the last week of his holiday in Paris, so that he might be in touch with his office. He was that much concerned about the matter.

But . . . 'When the stolid English go in for a scare,' he wrote later, 'they take leave of all moderation and commonsense. If nonsense were solid, the nonsense that was talked and written about those murders would sink a *Dreadnought*. The subject is an unsavoury one, and I must write about it with reserve. But it is enough to say that the wretched victims belonged to a very small class of degraded women who frequent the East End streets after midnight, in hope of inveigling belated drunkards or men as degraded as themselves. . . .'

It is probably the fact that prostitutes, only spoken of—if at all—in Victorian Society as 'unfortunates' or 'women of a certain class', achieved recognition as human beings through the publicity given to them over these murders. They certainly did achieve it then, and Dr. Anderson was therefore rather alone in taking the line that the subject could only be written about 'with reserve'. There was certainly little 'reserve' in the columns of the daily press in 1888, which dealt very fully with these women and their habits, and even printed quite sickening descriptions of their internal anatomy after Jack the Ripper had been at work on them.

In any case, Dr. Anderson's feeling that agitation over the murder of such people could be dismissed under the heading of 'nonsense' was not shared by the authorities.

So Dr. Anderson received, while he was in Paris, 'an urgent appeal' from the Home Secretary asking him to return to London and take up his job.

He did so—'Of course,' he says, 'I complied.'

On the night of his journey back, two prostitutes, named Elizabeth Stride and Catherine Eddowes, were murdered, one in a street in Whitechapel, and the other in a street in the neighbouring district of Aldgate.[1]

[1] This being within the boundaries of the City of London, the case was handled by the City Police and not by the Metropolitan Police.

9

'I spent the day of my return to town, and half the following night, in re-investigating the whole case, and next day I had a long conference on the subject with the Secretary of State and the Commissioner of Police.'

It may be imagined that the Home Secretary was not in any tranquil mood: those remarks about his 'helpless, heedless, useless figure' were still in his mind. Sir Charles Warren would not have been tranquil either, because of remarks about 'hopeless and conspicuous failure.' The extreme tranquillity of Dr. Anderson, edged with the freshness of mountain air from Switzerland, must therefore have been very trying for them.

So the interview did not have a very good start.

'"We hold you responsible to find the murderer" was Mr. Matthews' greeting to me. My answer was to decline the responsibility. "I hold myself responsible," I said, "to take all legitimate means to find him." But I went on to say that the measures I found in operation were, in my opinion, wholly indefensible and scandalous; for these wretched women were plying their trade under definite police protection.'

It is likely that the Home Secretary was not greatly interested in Dr. Anderson's opinion about that. For the function of the British Police is to protect all peaceable citizens who are not breaking the law: and what the Home Secretary wanted just then was the arrest, without delay, of someone who *was* breaking it—by murder.

But Dr. Anderson had a plan. '"Let the police of that district," I urged, "receive orders to arrest every known street woman found on the prowl after midnight."'

This action, which he considered would have been 'merciful to the very small class of women affected by it', because while in the cells they couldn't have been murdered, was 'deemed to be too drastic'. It would, in fact, have been illegal, for citizens of this country cannot be arrested unless they are believed to be breaking the law, and the law permits prostitutes to be 'on the prowl' provided they do not solicit.

Dr. Anderson therefore fell back on a second suggestion. '"Let us warn them that the police will not protect them."'

On the authority of his own statement, it appears that he was allowed to do that: and he did it. Though precisely what it meant is not clear. Hundreds of policemen remained in the district and it is not at all likely that one of them—whatever his orders about non-protection—would have stood quietly by, watching Jack the Ripper murder a woman and disembowel her.

10

Seven days later the Commissioner, Sir Charles Warren, resigned. There had been trouble all through his period of office, and it came to a head over 'work or bread' riots in Hyde Park by the unemployed. Sir Charles dealt drastically with that, even to the point of calling out a squadron of Life Guards (each with 20 rounds of ammunition) to support his 2,000 policemen. Then there were criticisms, and when it appeared that the Home Secretary was himself making criticisms in public, Warren was foolish enough to retort to them in a magazine article. He could, in fact, 'no longer brook the nagging ways'[1] of the Home Office

[1] Dr. (by that time Sir Robert) Anderson.

and resignation finally became the only possible course for him. Besides, there were those bloodhounds.

During the night following that resignation, a prostitute named Marie Jeanette Kelly[1] was murdered in a house in Whitechapel. Though even more horrible in the matter of disembowelling and mutilation, that murder was exactly like the others except for the fact that it was not committed in the open street, but in the victim's house:[2] and also for the fact that it was apparently committed in the morning, not at night. It was, in fact, the morning of Lord Mayor's Show day, and the vast crowds lining the streets were horrified when the newsboys shouted 'Another 'orrible murder in Whitechapel'.

Sir Charles Warren's resignation had not yet been

[1] It is not the function of this book to deal with the vexed question of the identity of Jack the Ripper, but only to deal with the conduct of Scotland Yard in trying to arrest him. But it may be mentioned here that there had been many theories about him: he is said to have been a seaman, a butcher, a policeman, a Malay, a doctor, a lunatic, etc. Dr. Anderson claims that 'the conclusion we came to was that he and his people were certain low-class Polish Jews. . . . And the result proved that our diagnosis was right on every point. For I may say at once that "undiscovered murders" are rare in London, and the Jack the Ripper crimes are not within that category.' There has, however, never been any official claim to that certainty: and indeed it has been contradicted by a high police official who took part in one of the enquiries.

One of the more interesting theories is that the Ripper was trying—for one reason or another—to kill a particular woman, but that beyond knowing that she was an East End prostitute (and perhaps knowing one of the names under which she had lived) he did not know enough to identify her; and that therefore he slaughtered five other women 'by mistake', before, in Marie Jeanette Kelly, he eventually found her. In that connection there is one point which does not seem hitherto to have been stressed. One of the earlier victims, Catherine Eddowes, had for the past seven years been living with one man, and (as was proved by his evidence and by the name on a dropped pawn-ticket) had been using his name. That name was Kelly. Thus all of the six victims had in common the fact that they were East End prostitutes; and two of the six had in common the fact that they lived under the name of Kelly.

[2] After explaining his plan for keeping the Whitechapel prostitutes off the streets, Dr. Anderson says, 'However the fact may be explained, it is a fact that no other street murder occurred.' The change in 'locale', however, did not make much difference to Marie Jeanette Kelly.

announced, so the newspapers again clamoured against him, as well as against the Home Secretary. They recorded the fact that Dr. Anderson 'drove up in a cab at ten minutes to two and remained some time' at the scene of the crime, and that Chief-Inspector Swanson of the Criminal Investigation Department was there as well as Inspector Abberline. But otherwise the enquiries proceeded according to the usual routine—and with the customary lack of result.

There was, in fact, nothing that Scotland Yard could do. This murderer left not a single clue, save the bodies of his victims. He appears to have been the one murderer who never made a mistake.

Marie Jeanette Kelly was the last woman he killed.[1] In due course, therefore, the outcry in the newspapers quietened down. Sir Charles Warren had been thrown to the wolves—or to his bloodhounds. But the Home Secretary survived, Dr. Anderson survived (to remain at his post for another six years, and then to retire with a K.C.B.)—and, although somewhat shaken and with an unhappy stain on its record of successes, the Criminal Investigation Department survived.

11

It was twenty-nine years since Constance Kent had murdered her brother. All the men who were at that time in the Detective Department at Great Scotland Yard had now gone, some by death, some by retirement, some to prison: the last, the most brilliant, the one who deserved fame although, as it happens, he has never really achieved

[1] It is presumably a coincidence that, a few months after the last of the murders in England, there was a closely similar outbreak in the West Indies, and a few months later still, another in South America.

it—Frederick Williamson—had retired as a very sick man. He died a few months later, in December 1889.

Thus ended an epoch. And it is perhaps fitting to close the record with the account from *The Times* of the funeral of this one man who had lived and worked through the whole of it. There had, as has been shown, been tragedies in his life, and he had become mistrustful, rather cynical, doubtful perhaps whether he had any friends. And yet——

'St. John's Church, Westminster, was yesterday the scene of a striking ceremony. Woking Cemetery had been selected as the burial place of the late Mr. Adolphus Frederick Williamson, Chief Constable of the Criminal Investigation Department of the Metropolitan Police; but a desire was expressed that the funeral service might be held in London, to enable the police of all ranks to render fitting respect to the memory of the deceased.

'From his house to the church, the coffin, wholly concealed by flowers, was carried by six of the inspectors of Scotland Yard, accompanied by the Assistant Commissioner and the Chief Constables of four of the London districts.

'The main body of the church was filled by officers of all ranks in the service, including nearly all the superintendents, and a large proportion of the inspectors of the Force. So general was the wish to be present that the attendance of sergeants and constables from the divisions had to be limited by order.'

12

The Criminal Investigation Department survived . . . it did, of course, do much more than merely 'survive'.

In the past twenty-nine years, the Detective Department, with its staff of eight men, had grown and developed into the C.I.D., with a staff of nearly 700 men: from being an unimportant and experimental offshoot of the Commissioners' Office, it had become, in its buildings at New Scotland Yard, the essential organisation in the war against crime.

Bibliography

The Times.
The Daily Telegraph.
The Daily News.
The Morning Post.
The Pall Mall Gazette.
The Western Daily News.
The Western Morning Press.
The Annual Register.
The London Figaro.
Scotland Yard, Past and Present—by ex-Chief-Inspector Tim Cavanagh.
The Reminiscences of Chief-Inspector Littlechild.
A Life's Reminiscences of Scotland Yard—by Arthur Lansdowne.
At Scotland Yard—by John Sweeney, C.I.D.
Mysteries of Police and Crime—by Arthur Griffiths.
The Lighter Side of my Official Life—by Sir Robert Anderson.
The Life of Sir Howard Vincent—by S. H. Jeyes & F. D. How.
Selected Speeches—by Sir Edward Clarke.

Bibliography

The Trial of Constance Kent—Edited by John Rhode.

The Trial of Kate Webster—Edited by Elliott O'Donnell.

The Trial of the Detectives—Edited by George Dilnot.

Scotland Yard—by George Dilnot.

Reprinted Pieces—by Charles Dickens.

Post Office Directories of London, 1860–1890.

Police Officers

(The rank given here is that last known to have been held during the period covered by this book)

Abberline, Insp. F.G.
Anderson, Dr. Robert
Butcher, Chief-Inspector
Cavanagh, Insp. Timothy
Clarke, Ch.-Insp. George
Cobb, Sergeant
Cole, Constable George
Davey, Inspector
Diffey, Mrs. Martha
Dowdell, Insp. John
Druscovich, Ch.-Insp. Nathaniel
Eccles, Inspector
Glass, Inspector
Godley, Sergeant
Greenham, Chief-Inspector
Harber, Inspector
Henderson, Col. Edmund
Howie, Superintendent
Jones, Inspector
Kerrissey, Inspector
Lansdowne, Insp. Arthur
Littlechild, Chief-Inspector
McCarthy, Sergeant
Mayne, Sir Richard
Meiklejohn, Insp. John
Monro, James
Moore, Inspector
Mulvaney, Inspector
Nairn, Inspector
Neame, Chief-Inspector
O'Callaghan, Inspector
Palmer, Chief-Inspector William
Pay, Inspector
Pearce, Sergeant
Pearman, Inspector
Reid, Inspector
Richardson, Inspector
Robinson, Sergeant
Rowan, Sir Charles
Sayer, Inspector
Searle, Inspector
Shore, Supt. John

Police Officers

Shrives, Sergeant
Steer, Inspector
Stroud, Sergeant
Swanson, Chief-Inspector
Tanner, Inspector Richard
Thicke, Sergeant
Thomas, Sergeant
Thomson, Supt. James J.
Thornton, Insp. Stephen
Tiddy, Superintendent
Vincent, Howard
Von Tornow, Inspector
Warren, Sir Charles
Whicher, Insp. Jonathan
Williamson, Chief Constable Frederick

For details, see Index

Index

Index

Index